INSTANT
INDIAN

Classic Foods from Every Region of India
Made Easy in the **Instant Pot**®

Rinku Bhattacharya

Hippocrene Books, Inc.
New York

For further information, contact:
HIPPOCRENE BOOKS, INC.
171 Madison Avenue
New York, NY 10016
www.hippocrenebooks.com

INSTANT POT and associated logos are owned by Double Insight, Inc. Used under license.

Library of Congress Cataloging-in-Publication Data

Names: Bhattacharya, Rinku, author.
Title: Instant Indian : classic foods from every region of India made easy in the Instant
    Pot / Rinku Bhattacharya.
Description: New York : Hippocrene Books, Inc., [2018] | Includes index.
Identifiers: LCCN 2018028312| ISBN 9780781813853 (pbk.) | ISBN 0781813859 (pbk.)
Subjects: LCSH: Cooking, Indic. | Pressure cooking. | Electric cooking. | LCGFT:
    Cookbooks.
Classification: LCC TX724.5.I4 B4993 2018 | DDC 641.5954--dc23
LC record available at https://lccn.loc.gov/2018028312

Book design by Brittany Hince and K & P Publishing

Printed in the United States of America.

INSTANT
INDIAN

CONTENTS

Introduction

There are few modern tools that have survived the test of generations in an Indian kitchen. Over time we have grudgingly replaced the grinding stone with the electric grinder and the hand grater with the food processor, however, the pressure cooker retains its place of pride. It was an essential tool in my grandmother's kitchen, in fact her main pressure cooker endured thirty years of everyday use. Of course my mother used hers, and in my kitchen I too have had an assortment of pressure cookers—the first one arrived as a wedding gift from my mother-in-law. I began consistently using it once my children were born, beginning with making baby food in minutes, then homemade chicken broth, and finally moving to nourishing lentil and rice stews called *khichuri*.

My kitchen is the central hub of activity in our house, usually the room I first enter once I come home from work and catch up with the children. The hum of the pressure cooker is a consistent sound, almost like the rhythm of the kitchen. This steamy song links the sounds of my Indian childhood with those of my children growing up several continents away.

Stews dominate the Indian table, in the form of curries and dals, and the pressure cooker is the Indian home cook's tool to ensure that dals are meltingly soft and meats comfortingly tender. Many people refer to the pressure cooker as simply "cooker." Other staples on the Indian table, such as whole grains, porridges, compotes, and steamed desserts all fit beautifully into the pressure cooker universe. From a practical standpoint, the pressure cooker is well-suited to the Indian kitchen, where cooks are conscious about energy usage and, like everyone else, need their dinner in a hurry.

The heavy-bottomed base of the pressure cooker allows for the preparation of the curry or spice base, and often results in converting Indian dishes into the much coveted one-pot meal. In fact, it is this very distinction that makes the pressure cooker more of a natural in the Indian kitchen, in contrast to the slow cooker. At the heart of Indian cooking is tempering, slowly browning spices and onions, without which the rich flavor of Indian foods are incomplete. Of course, when speaking of the depth of flavor, it is certainly worth mentioning that pressure cooking retains more flavor and allows you to cook with a lot less fat. To obtain subtleness of texture, it is important to be able to control the temperature at varying levels during the cooking process.

A couple of years ago, I purchased an Instant Pot® brand electric multi-function cooker, intending to use it mostly for slow cooking. However, once I discovered timed "fix and forget" pressure cooking, there has been no going back—it has been instant love! I learned how to adapt all of my tried-and-true recipes for this much-loved device and we are a happy family. We traded the gentle hum and hiss of the stove top for the beeps and numerical countdown of the Instant Pot®. I am thrilled to be able to re-create all our usual favorites, most in less than thirty minutes, without compromising flavors. And rather than resorting to the takeout menu, we have easy and satisfying dals, chana masala, and butter chicken all at our finger tips. In fact, if you are already comfortable with a pressure cooker, the electric pressure cooker will make you quite delirious. It dramatically reduces the active time needed as it cooks and shuts down on its own, requiring no babysitting.

My goal with this book is to offer you a broad foundation of Indian cuisine adapted for the Instant Pot® and then let you decide how you want to adapt and incorporate them into your own life. To assist you in this journey I have used the Instant Pot® to simplify the recipes without compromising their authenticity. My selection of recipes has been at the cusp of nostalgic and traditional. There are favorites like the ones that bring students into my kitchen, and family heirlooms that take you on a journey around India. You will also find recipes for most Indian restaurant staples, ranging from Butter Chicken to Vindaloo, Chana Masala to Aloo Gobi, holding court alongside homey dishes like an Assamese Egg and Potato Curry. I have long wanted to write a book showcasing the cultural diversity of Indian cooking and at the same time, keeping it easy and accessible for everyone. Thanks to Instant Pot® I have been able to do just that.

Two features of the Instant Pot® that are best-suited for Indian cooking are the pressure cooking and the steaming functions. I have never been able to steam as effectively with other devices as I can with the Instant Pot®. Traditional steamed dishes such as Idlis (Rice Cakes), Dhoklas (Chickpea Flour Cakes), and Bhapa Doi Shorse Maach (Steamed Salmon with Mustard and Poppy Seeds) are all now easily accessible for a weeknight meal. Then there is getting truly creative—the Yogurt setting works wonders for yogurt of course, but in addition it provides the absolutely perfect temperature to ferment traditional South Indian dosa and idli batter, and believe it or not for sprouting legumes in less than 24 hours. With this function, the possibilities are endless.

I also offer you tips throughout the book on planning and simplifying so you can incorporate your favorite Indian dishes into your weeknight mealtime rotation—a challenge I live with almost every day of my life! I am a busy commuter working mom, who has learned to conquer the weekday meal challenge with some planning ahead. A lot of the tips in this book are ones that I wish someone had given me years and years ago! Think of this as an authentic girlfriend's guide to Indian cooking.

And speaking of friends, one of the best things about the Instant Pot® is that it has inspired many online groups and they help us form a community. My cookbook has its very own Facebook community where I and others share recipes and tips—Instant Pot® Regional Indian Recipes and Cooking. In addition, there are always recipes, ideas, and more on my blog "Spice Chronicles." I look forward to seeing you there!

—Rinku

About the Instant Pot®

An Instant Pot® is a great fun addition to any kitchen. Before you get to my recipes using the Instant Pot®, it is a good idea to read the manufacturer's manual. There is also a lot of useful information on the Instant Pot® website (instantpot.com), including short video tutorials that will get you familiar with the features of the Instant Pot®.

REMEMBER IT IS A MULTICOOKER:
There are some important things to remember when jumping onto the Instant Pot® bandwagon for Indian cooking. The Pressure Cooking function of the Instant Pot® is well-suited to Indian recipes, and probably the one you'll use most often. However, there are various other features of the Instant Pot® that are very useful in the Indian kitchen and learning to use them through my recipes will help you get more mileage from this device. The recipes in this cookbook use the Rice setting, Steam setting, and Yogurt setting extensively as these work very well in many Indian recipes.

INSTANT IS AS INSTANT DOES:
Despite its very catchy name, cooking in the Instant Pot® is not literally instantaneous. If you are used to using a pressure cooker, this might be a little disappointing. However, overall you do save a lot of time, because the Instant Pot® needs very little hands-on time for cooking. This is the crux of Instant Pot® magic for me. Overall things do take less time to make than conventional stove-top cooking. Once you get used to features such as the delayed start, you will be able to schedule your cooking so it starts at your convenience and food is ready when you need it.

WHICH INSTANT POT® MODEL TO BUY:
The Instant Pot® company is committed to ever-evolving and finding ways to up the ante with its device. I will therefore caution you not to ditch your current model for the newest model if you really do not need to. My recipes have been tested on the Duo, Duo Plus, and Ultra. I

think these models all work well and offer the multi-functionality that is needed for the recipes in this book. There are just a handful of no pressure steam recipes that can only be done in the Ultra. If you own the Lux, you will have to play around a little. The Lux does not have the adjustable temperature settings and several of my recipes use low pressure cooking. In addition it also does not have a Yogurt setting. Having said that, there are plenty of recipes in this book that will work with the Lux. I also made my instructions generic enough that you can try the recipes with other multi-cooker brands.

GETTING REAL WITH THE TIME:

The Instant Pot® is quite the phenomenon because it cuts down on time and practically cooks unattended. This is a huge timesaver. Having said that, it is important to note that most recipes will take longer than just the pressure cooking time. You need to factor in the time it takes to come to full pressure, the actual pressure cooking time, and the time for steam release. I have accounted for the complete cooking cycle by noting a total time needed with all my recipes. The timing for some of these recipes might seem lengthy, but you should keep in mind that in most cases the hands-on active time is indeed almost instant.

INSTANT POT® SETTINGS AND THEIR USE IN THE INSTANT INDIAN KITCHEN

The sheer number of buttons on the Instant Pot® models can be quite complex and confusing. My first word of advice is to learn the basics before you make the pre-set buttons work for you. Not all the Instant Pot® buttons are used in this book, so I will walk you through the ones that I have commonly used in my recipes.

Manual/Pressure Cook: This is the basic button. The plus and minus keys allow you to increase or decrease the time, with the lowest setting being zero. Typically you'll use the High Pressure setting. However, the Low Pressure setting is great for cooking more delicate items such as fish or vegetables.

Sauté setting: The Sauté setting is used at the start of recipes to heat the oil and brown the spices, onions, ginger, garlic, and other base ingredients that are needed at the beginning of almost every one of my recipes, since in Indian cooking sizzling or blooming spices in oil is often how a recipe begins. It is important to let the oil heat at least a minute or two before adding the whole spices. Do not be daunted when the Instant Pot® says hot.

Cancel: This button is used for turning off the Instant Pot®. Several of my recipes begin with sautéing and then move over to some kind of pressure cooking and the cancel button is used in these instances for switching modes.

Rice setting: The Instant Pot® does a wonderful job of cooking complex rice dishes like magic. The Rice setting is a fully automated low pressure mode pre-set at 12 minutes. The most common variable here is the water to rice ratio. In the rice chapter I have tried to account for most of the common varieties of rice used in the Indian kitchen (see pages 63-64).

Steam setting: Steam cooking uses pressure in all models except the Ultra. If you own the Ultra, my recommendation is to use the Steam setting without pressure for steaming the breakfast items. The other dishes in this book use the traditional Steam setting. The use of water allows for gentle moist cooking.

Yogurt setting: The Yogurt setting in the Instant Pot® defaults to 8 hours of low heat. This helps in setting yogurt. It also allows for perfect fermentation and sprouting of beans and legumes.

OTHER TERMINOLOGY:

As with all tools and devices, the Instant Pot® has built its own culinary terminology:

IP or Instapot: These are often other names or shorthand for the Instant Pot®. These terms are loosely used for other electric multicookers as well.

High Pressure (HP): High Pressure is the default cooking mode for several of the preset programs and is used for many recipes in this cookbook.

Low Pressure (LP): Low Pressure is the default cooking mode for programs such as the rice setting.

Quick (Pressure) Release (QR / QPR): Refers to the process of opening the valve to release steam quickly, to prevent the contents from cooking further.

Natural (Pressure) Release (NP / NPR): This process can take 10 to 20 minutes and allows the pressure to release on its own once the cooking time has lapsed.

Pressure Cooking Time Tables

Dried Beans, Legumes & Lentils	DRY Cooking Time (minutes)	SOAKED Cooking Time (minutes)
Adzuki beans	16 - 20	4 - 6
Black beans	20 - 25	6 - 8
Black-eyed peas	14 - 18	4 - 5
Cannellini beans	30 - 35	6 - 9
Chickpeas (garbanzo bean)	35 - 40	10 - 15
Great Northern beans	25 - 30	7 - 8
Kidney beans, red	20 - 25	7 - 8
Lentils, brown	8 - 10	n/a
Lentils, green	8 - 10	n/a
Lentils, red, split	1 - 2	n/a
Lentils, yellow, split	1 - 2	n/a
Lima beans	12 - 14	6 - 10
Navy beans	20 - 25	7 - 8
Peas	16 - 20	10 - 12
Pinto beans	25 - 30	6 - 9

Meat (Poultry, Lamb, & Pork)	Cooking Time (minutes)
Chicken, breasts (boneless)	6 - 8
Chicken, cut with bones	10 - 15
Turkey, breast (boneless)	7 - 9
Lamb, cubes	10 - 15
Lamb, leg	15 / 450 g / 1 lb
Lamb, stew meat	12 - 15
Pork, butt roast	15 / 450 g / 1 lb
Pork, ribs	15 - 20

Seafood & Fish	FRESH Cooking Time (minutes)	FROZEN Cooking Time (minutes)
Crab, whole	2 - 3	4 - 5
Fish, fillet	2 - 3	3 - 4
Fish, steak	3 - 4	4 - 6
Fish, whole	4 - 5	5 - 7
Seafood soup or stock	7 - 8	8 - 9
Shrimp or Prawn	1 - 3	2 - 4

A Few Notes on Using this Cookbook

Dairy substitutions: If you want to use a substitute for dairy items in a recipe, soy yogurt is a good alternative to yogurt, and coconut milk is a good alternative to cream.

Dietary Information: All recipes in this book have been coded as appropriate, if they fall into these categories:

VG	**V**	**GF**
Vegan	Vegetarian	Gluten-free

Timing: I have divided the times needed into Sauté Time, Pressure Cook Time, Pressure Release Time and then give the Total Time. The Total Time accounts for the time needed for the recipes to reach pressure and resting and prep time. This allows you to plan your time accordingly.

Temperatures: The default Sauté mode or Pressure mode cooking temperature in this book is high, when a low or medium setting is needed it has been specified in the recipe.

0 Minute: Setting the Instant Pot® to Pressure Cook for 0 Minute (Pressing "Manual/Pressure Cook" Button, then adjust to "0" minute) means the Instant Pot® will get up to pressure, then immediately switch off. The food will be cooked during the "coming up to pressure" time.

THE DIVERSITY OF INDIAN COOKING:

Regions, Spices & Kitchen Basics

Geography, Culture, Religion and the Indian Table

Indian cooking is complex, eclectic, and evolving. It involves several culinary influences folded in one, making the cuisine fascinating and richly nuanced. Regional influences in India are shaped both by the topography and the culture. It is inherently a very sustainable and eco-friendly cuisine, and many foods and techniques have evolved around what is readily available in the region. Indian restaurants often present dishes as a uniform amalgamated cuisine, but this is far from true. For example, I am from Eastern India while my husband is North Indian, and our culinary heritages have distinct differences.

This said, the style and essential techniques of Indian cooking unite the body of food called Indian cuisine. Indian meals are rarely served in multiple courses, which is why the formal style of plating involves a *thali* , a large plate with multiple small bowls to separate the different items. Indian food is well-seasoned with a multitude of spices (this does not necessarily mean it is spicy in terms of heat), and a complete meal is usually a balanced affair including carbohydrates (rice or flatbreads), lentils, vegetables, proteins, and frequently dessert. There is often an assortment of relishes and yogurt served on the side.

Culinary traditions are most influenced by what is readily available in the region. This explains the extensive use of seafood and coconut in coastal cuisines, the use of lentils and legumes in the drier western parts of India, and of course the use of mustard and leafy greens in eastern India. The culinary traditions of neighboring countries have also spilled into the cuisine of India. For example there are a lot of Chinese influences in the cooking of northeast India as well as the northern highlands of Ladakh.

Cultural influences are comprised of religion, colonialism, and trade. India is a land of almost every imaginable religion. With Hinduism restricting beef and Islam restricting pork, not surprisingly the common red meat of choice is non-controversial goat meat. I have substituted lamb for a lot of goat dishes in this book, however, the preferred meat of choice in the Indian kitchen is goat. Every religion has its own unique imprint on Indian cooking. The Jain table presents us with a rich, flavorful range of cooking that is made completely without onions and garlic. Classic communal-style dishes such as Langar Ki Dal (page 103) are found on the Sikh table, as the Sikh temples offer free meals to anyone who chooses to eat there.

Trade and colonialism have also enriched and influenced the Indian table. The Portuguese introduced spices such as the red pepper as well as tomatoes. The distinct influences of

Portuguese cooking can be found in the state of Goa, a former Portuguese colony. Similarly, you can find French influences in the cuisine of Pondicherry. There is an entire culinary repertoire termed "Anglo-Indian," or the cuisine of the Raj, as it evolved during the British reign over India. In fact, Indian food is extremely popular in Britain and some of the best Indian food outside India can be found there.

Restaurants and home cooks are beginning to move beyond well-known dishes such as Tikka Masala and Korma, now delving further into the treasure trove that is Indian cooking. As with all cuisines, authenticity has many dimensions. There are complex heirloom recipes holding court alongside simple homestyle dishes that are hearty, full-flavored, and very easy to make. This cookbook assures you authentic recipes—a little taste of every region of India— carefully chosen to be practical and suitable for a busy lifestyle.

FOUR BROAD REGIONAL CLASSIFICATIONS

North Indian Cuisine: This is the cuisine of the states of Uttar Pradesh, Himachal, Uttarkhand, Delhi, Punjab, and Central India. It is the mainstream cuisine found in many restaurants outside India. North Indian cuisine can be vegetarian or non-vegetarian and typically uses a lot of dairy. There are Mughal influences that include nuts and dried fruit, and culinary techniques such as grilling, particularly in the tandoori oven. North Indian cuisine also showcases a variety of breads, such as naan or paratha.

Western Indian Cuisine: This is the cuisine of Maharastra, Gujarat, Goa, and part of Rajasthan. The coastal location of Maharastra trailing down to South India feature a well-seasoned cuisine rich in fish and coconut milk that is also called Konkani cuisine. This moves into Goa, where fish and coconut milk are featured alongside a distinct Portuguese influence, particularly the use of garlic, chilies, and vinegar. The cuisine of Gujarat is mostly vegetarian, and dishes often include a hint of sweetness.

Eastern Indian Cuisine: The culinary heritage of eastern India brings together the states of West Bengal and Orrisa. Eight northeastern states—Sikkim, Manipur, Meghalaya, Assam, Arunachal Pradesh, Tripura, Mizoram, and Nagaland—also fall into this broad classification. The cuisine of these states is unique in its incorporation of herbs and Chinese ingredients. The culinary heritage of eastern India is rich in leafy greens, mustard, fish, and seafood. They also use milk to make chenna/paneer (a fresh white cheese) found in many desserts.

South Indian Cuisine: This is the cuisine of the states of Tamil Nadu, Karnataka, Kerala, and Telangana. The cuisine of South India features rice, lentils, and characteristic favorites like *idlis* and *dosas*, often collectively grouped as *tiffin*. The seasonings are bold, with generous use of coconut and curry leaves. Famous in southern India are lentil stews such as Sambhar (page 100) and *kottus*.

The Instant Indian Kitchen

At the heart of Indian cooking are spices and herbs. I have tried my best to keep the spices and herbs used in this book to a few key essentials. Beyond taste, the benefits and the practical uses of these spices and herbs are rooted in the tradition of Ayurveda (Indian holistic medicine). The Ayurvedic tradition of cooking comes from a 14th-century ancient Indian text, or veda, that is the prescription or base of Indian cuisine.

I am fond of using fresh ingredients like ginger, garlic, and herbs rather than an excessive amount of spices to season my food. The staple ingredients in my cooking are fresh ginger and garlic and loads of cilantro, lemon, cumin seeds, and black pepper. I also encourage you to try my recipes with freshly ground spices, as they impart more flavor. It is a good idea to invest in a sturdy coffee or spice grinder for this purpose.

In terms of Indian brands for products and spice blends, there are several good options. I personally tend to favor MTR Foods Private Limited Spices or Everest Spices. Swad brand, manufactured by Raja Foods in Skokie, Illinois, also offers a comprehensive array of products.

The Indian spice box (*masala dani*), usually a large round container holding five or six smaller ones, is designed to store your most essential spices. These essentials can vary from chef to chef, but the spice box takes care of two key needs: accessibility and air-free and moisture-free storage. It is essential to keep spices in airtight containers to retain their flavor.

GLOSSARY OF SPICES, AROMATICS AND HERBS

Asafoetida: Asafoetida (also called "hing") is a pungent spice used in cooking, in addition to being consumed as a digestive aid. Native to Central Asia, particularly Iran and India, asafoetida comes from a very unusual source. It is made by scraping the sap from the exposed root of a plant in the carrot family. The sap is dried and crushed, giving us a tan-colored powder to sprinkle into our dishes. It is most commonly used in vegetarian recipes, sometimes as a replacement for onion and garlic. Its pungent smell can make this powder seem off-putting, but rest assured it dissipates while cooking, bringing a full, savory flavor to foods.

Bay Leaves (Tejpata): These aromatic leaves have a fragrance similar to cinnamon. The Indian bay leaf is distinct and different from the smaller western bay laurel leaf. The fragrance is also stronger. These leaves are dried and used extensively to add a touch of fragrant sweetness to stews, desserts and rice dishes.

Cardamom: The fragrant pod of the cardamom plant in the Zingiberaceae family, cardamom is native to the Indian sub-continent. The two most common variations are the sage green, spindle-shaped green cardamom and the dark brown or black husky cardamom.

Carom Seeds: These are tiny brown seeds known as *ajwain* in Hindi and Bengali. They are used sparingly to offer a gentle touch of assertiveness. If unavailable you can substitute with dried or fresh thyme leaves.

Cayenne pepper, dried whole: Cayenne peppers are the chilies most commonly used in Indian kitchens. These long slender chilies, named after the town of Cayenne in French Guyana, are usually ripened until red and then dried. Dried whole red chilies are mostly used for flavor and sometimes even appearance since they do not offer a lot of heat when added as a whole spice to recipes. For more heat, the dried red chili is also crushed and made into red chili powder or cayenne pepper powder (see below). I also enjoy using dried red pepper flakes, often as a garnish to offer a rougher distribution of heat.

Cayenne pepper powder: Dried red cayenne peppers are often ground into what is known as red chili powder or cayenne pepper powder. Its heat makes an Indian dish complete. Cayenne pepper powder is portable and convenient to keep around since it does not spoil. (Note: the mixture found in mainstream U.S. stores labeled "chili powder" is a spice blend distinct and different from what I describe here.)

Chaat masala: Chaat masala is a sweet, tangy and somewhat spicy seasoning blend from North India. It is mainly used in the North Indian street salads called *chaat*. I use it in certain recipes to capture the same spicy tangy kick.

Cilantro: Cilantro leaves (also called coriander and Chinese parsley) are very versatile. It is the herb of choice in the Indian kitchen, with mint being a close second. My joke is that we use cilantro as a green vegetable in our house. It is a perennial plant that grows one to two feet high and features dark green, hairless, soft leaves that are variable in shape. The leaves and stems have a light citrus flavor. It packs a strong dose of antioxidants, minerals, and vitamins, and is of course low in calories. Be forewarned, however, that there are a host of people to whom cilantro tastes like soap.

Cinnamon: A spice obtained from the inner bark of several tree species from the plant species *Cinnamomum*. Cinnamon is used mainly as an aromatic condiment and flavoring addition in a wide variety of cuisines. In Indian cuisine, it is used mostly in delicate savory dishes such as fragrant rice dishes and it is also a common ingredient of the fragrant spice blend Garam Masala.

Cloves: These are the aromatic flower buds of a tree in the plant family Myrtaceae. They are native to the Maluku Islands (or Moluccas) in Indonesia. Cloves have a sharper almost astringent flavor and are used in the same way as cinnamon. Cloves are also used in spice blends for lentils and beans.

Coriander seeds: These small brown seeds, used either whole or crushed, are native to Europe and North Africa and belong to the coriander plant. Coriander is the word used to describe both the seeds and the fresh herb in most places but in the U.S. we use the Spanish word "cilantro" for the fresh herb. I personally like the distinction though this difference in names often masks the fact that the two ingredients are related. Coriander seeds are rarely used as a sole flavoring. Coriander, with its softer flavor is most commonly used to compliment and round off the flavors of other stronger spices such as cumin and black pepper. The recipes in this book are made with freshly ground coriander seeds, which makes a much stronger spice than the pre-made commercial varieties.

Cumin seeds: Cumin is native to Middle Eastern and Mediterranean regions. It was grown in ancient Egypt where the seeds were used in rituals and to season food. It comes in varieties of white, brown, and black. There are differences in taste depending on the color and type of cumin used. In my kitchen, I typically use the brown variety. Cumin is also used in powdered form. The recipes in this book are made with freshly ground cumin seeds, which makes a much stronger spice than the pre-made commercial varieties.

Curry leaves: These strong-smelling leaves of the kari or curry leaf tree are ironically the only item in the Indian kitchen actually named "curry." Curry leaves freeze well and impart an unmistakable fragrance to both stews and stir-fries. They add a nice depth of flavor, especially to creamy coconut-based sauces. Try bruising a leaf to inhale the luscious aroma.

Dried Mango Powder: Sold as amchur in Indian markets, this powder imparts a gentle tang. It is made from unripe mangoes, dried and then ground for use in dishes. It is different from lime or lemon although they can be substituted in a bind.

Fennel seeds: Fennel seeds are a sweet anise-like spice. They are one of the few spices eaten raw as a mouth freshener. They are an essential spice for some pickle and chutney recipes, and I like to add them to some basic curries as well.

Fenugreek leaves: Both the seeds and leaves of the fenugreek plant have culinary uses. A winter staple in India, fresh fenugreek greens are very nutritious. I've found that fresh fenugreek greens in the U.S. do not have the characteristic faintly maple flavor of their Indian counterparts. However, dried fenugreek leaves called *kasuri methi* are readily available and more reliable in terms of flavor. This is one of the exceptions in my kitchen where I tend to use the dried leaves more often than fresh ones, however they cannot always be used interchangeably. Fenugreek is what gives commercial curry powder mixes their characteristic "curry" flavor.

Garam Masala: A fragrant blend of aromatic spices, the garam masala blend is best made at home (see recipe on page 31), or alternately bought in small quantities to use as needed.

Garlic: Garlic is a species in the onion family. Its close relatives include onions, shallots, leeks, and chives. Dating back over six thousand years, garlic is native to central Asia and has long been a staple in the Mediterranean region, as well as a frequently used seasoning in Asia, Africa, and Europe. Garlic can be ground with fresh ginger in equal portions to create a ginger-garlic paste (page 35). Fresh ginger-garlic paste will keep in the refrigerator for up to two weeks, and it can also be stored in the freezer almost indefinitely.

Ginger: Fresh ginger is really a rhizome that is often referred to as a root. This rhizome belongs to the ginger plant. The brown skin is peeled to reveal a pale yellow inside. The sharp, fragrant root is usually grated or ground into a paste. Ginger also works as a twin spice with garlic. Ginger-garlic paste (page 35) can be made in large amounts in the blender and then frozen in small amounts (try using an ice cube tray) to be used as needed.

Green Chili Peppers: The small green chili pepper is sold in many varieties. In Asian supermarkets, they are sold as Vietnamese chilies; then there is the unripe, green fruit of the cayenne tree, the cayenne pepper; and then the family of American peppers including the Serrano, jalapeno, and habanero. For the recipes in this book—other than not substituting green chilies with red ones—I usually leave it up to you what type of green chili you use depending on how much heat you want.

Kashmiri Red Chili Pepper: There is a whole assortment of ground Indian peppers that range from a gentle heat to an almost sweet taste. The most common of these is sold as *deghi mirch*. I often use ground ancho peppers or sweet paprika as a substitute. My favorite are the wrinkled chilies from Southern India, sold as *byadagi*; if you find them, try using them freshly ground. You will love the combination of their fresh fragrance and mild heat. The other Indian contender is the vividly red Kashmiri red chili pepper, which has a dazzling, vibrant color with just a hint of sweetness. But while each of the sweeter pepper varieties do have their unique flavors, in most cases they are being added for color and any readily available sweet pepper powder such as paprika can be substituted.

Mint: Mint is the most popular herb in Indian cooking after cilantro, particularly in northern India. I often recommend it as a substitute for cilantro in recipes for a variation, but you should note that mint has a strong taste and should be used in smaller amounts than cilantro. It is most popularly used in marinades, smooth pesto-like chutneys, and flatbreads. In a bind, powdered mint can be used; I like dried varieties from Middle Eastern stores the best.

Mustard seeds: Common mustard seeds come in black and yellow varieties. The yellow mustard seed is better suited to someone who finds the taste of fresh ground mustard too strong. I use black mustard seeds for most of the recipes in this book. When added to oil, mustard seeds crackle and transform, the seeds turning darker and nutty.

Nigella seeds: These shiny black seeds have a characteristic onion-like flavor. They are used for sautéing vegetables, finishing lentils, and for pressing into bread to offer some colorful contrast.

Panch Phoron / Bengali Five Spice Mixture: This is a mixture from eastern India comprised of equal parts fennel seeds, mustard seeds, fenugreek seeds, cumin seeds, and nigella seeds. It is available premixed and is a great spice for tempering and stir-frying dishes.

Peppercorns: The black peppercorn is the fruit of a flowering vine that is native to Southern India and Sri Lanka. The assorted colors of the peppercorn—white, green, and black—are really different degrees of ripeness and result in varying degrees of heat. Black pepper powder is the ground-up version of black peppercorns and is one of the most commonly used spices in the world. A peppermill is worth its weight in flavor, so it is very important to have one around for introducing the spark of freshly ground black pepper to food.

Tamarind: This dark sticky fruit is from the tamarind tree. In its natural form tamarind is used as a souring agent for cooking purposes. As a condiment, however, sweet and sour tamarind chutney is very popular and used as a dressing to complement other spicy chutneys. Particularly in the cuisine of southern India, tamarind is the traditional souring agent. Currently tamarind is available in markets as a strained and prepared paste. This form offers freshness and convenience.

Tandoori Masala: A savory spice blend that's relatively easy to make at home (see recipe on page 34). You can also buy it readymade in small quantities.

Turmeric: Turmeric is a rhizome, not unlike ginger. It is popularly used in Indian cooking in a dried and powdered form. I like to call it "trendy" turmeric as it seems to be the happening spice these days because of all its health benefits. Indeed, it is an anti-inflammatory spice that is supposed to prevent cancer, offer the skin a glow, and of course, add flavor and color to your food.

FATS AND OILS

Here I outline the fats and oils that are suitable for use in my recipes. If you are vegan, the clarified butter called for in some of my vegetarian recipes can be replaced with one of these oils.

Canola oil: Canola oil is the workhorse of most Indian kitchens. Its neutral taste, high smoking point, and lack of saturated fat make it a practical choice for everyday cooking. Depending on your preference, this oil can effectively be used for most of the recipes in this book. There has been some concern lately that canola oil might be being made from GMO seeds. If this is of concern to you, grapeseed oil is a good substitute.

Coconut oil: Traditionally coconut oil is used in South Indian cuisine. These days it is considered very beneficial and hence its huge popularity. It is a dense shelf stable oil, and I use it as a substitute for ghee in vegetarian dishes to keep them vegan.

Ghee: Clarified butter with the water and milk solids drained out is a concentrated form of butter called ghee. It is used in Indian cooking as well as Middle Eastern cuisine in lieu of butter. I use it in moderation as a little goes a long way to add a nutty rich flavor or finish. (See recipe page 27.)

Grapeseed oil: This light-tasting oil is found in most supermarkets these days and is almost always available in Mediterranean stores. I tend to use this for shallow frying and anything that needs higher temperatures, since it has a higher smoking point than olive oil. I use grapeseed oil more often than canola or olive oil, since it is healthier and its milder taste works better with most Indian dishes. The best variety of grapeseed oil has a clean finish and a pale green color.

Mustard oil: Because of the supposed toxicity of erucic acid that is found in mustard oil, it has become a controversial ingredient for cooking in the United States, and tends to be sold in its purest form and labeled "for external use only." But since erucic acid is also found in canola oil (just in smaller doses), and mustard oil has been used in Indian cooking for centuries without any detrimental effects, I still use it. There are some recipes where I like and crave the distinct, sharp taste of this oil. I am comfortable with using pure mustard oil, and in fact, I grew up eating food cooked in it. If you are troubled by the labeling, however, there are mustard oil blends (like the one made by SWAD) that offer most of the flavor of pure mustard oil.

MAKE-AHEAD BASICS

In addition to stocking your pantry with a good balance of spices, lentils, rice, and essential oils, there are a few foods that are used in or served with most Indian dishes. A lot of these are not made in an Instant Pot®, but rest assured they will make your Instant Pot® recipes delicious. Essential curry spice blend and pastes and freshly grated ginger and garlic are used in a lot of Indian cooking. I make batches of these at the beginning of the week to save time later. Silicon egg molds (available at online retailers) can hold about half a cup of essential curry pastes and are convenient for storing them. (We have put each of the spice pastes as a heading in the Index in case you're looking for recipes that use a pre-made paste.)

Essential Plain Yogurt

———

Yogurt is a staple in the Indian kitchen. It is used in cooking, for drinks such as Lassi (page 228), and in a savory salad like Raita (page 239). In many Indian homes yogurt is eaten to finish a meal. It is easy, practical, and economical to make yogurt in your Instant Pot®. I deviate a little from making this completely in the Instant Pot® as I have found it quicker to heat the milk on the stove-top or even the microwave first.

A Few Notes:

• *A good starter or active culture is essential. The batch that has been going strong for me started with Trader Joe's Greek Yogurt. I like it because when we travel or something happens and my starter is gone I have something to fall back on.*

• *The right temperature: I use a thermometer for this and it has been well worth it. The right temperature for me has been about 125 degrees F.*

• *I have actually found using a metal non-reactive container works better than ceramic glass ones.*

MAKES	TOTAL TIME: 8 HOURS & 15 MINUTES	DIETARY
2 cups	Prep Time: 5 minutes Cool Time: 10 minutes Yogurt Setting: 8 hours	

INGREDIENTS

2 cups whole or low-fat (2%) milk

3 tablespoons organic yogurt starter (organic plain yogurt)

INSTRUCTIONS

1. Heat the milk in a small saucepan on the stovetop until it reaches a simmer. Place in a container with a lid. Cool until its temperature is about 125 degrees F.

2. Place the milk in a non-reactive container (a stainless steel container with a lid is great for this purpose). Mix in the starter. Cover the container and place in the Instant Pot®. Place the cover on and select the Yogurt setting. After 8 hours your yogurt will be ready. Refrigerate a few hours before eating.

Homemade Evaporated Milk

Evaporated milk is often used in Instant Pot® cooking. I was introduced to canned evaporated milk early in my life in the United States. I use it in a bind, however, I really have a hard time using it in Indian desserts. It is nothing like the rich, creamy, thickened product we get by reducing milk. Thickened milk, or ghono dudh as we call it in Bengali, is the key to making rich Indian sweets. The steady temperature of the Instant Pot® Sauté mode set on medium is higher than what I'd use on the stove top but allows you to comfortably cook down the milk without much fuss or attention. The thickened milk will keep in the refrigerator for five days and can be frozen for later use.

MAKES	TOTAL TIME: 50 MINUTES	DIETARY
1¾ cups	Sauté Time: 45 minutes	

INGREDIENTS
½ gallon whole milk

INSTRUCTIONS

1. Place the milk in the Instant Pot®. Set the Instant Pot® on Sauté mode with medium heat.

2. Stir once when the milk reaches a boiling temperature.

3. After 5 minutes, it should achieve the thickness of most commercial evaporated milk. After an additional 30 minutes, it works for most Indian dishes.

Paneer/Chenna
Indian White Cheese

Commercially-made paneer is readily available and can be used for any of the savory recipes in this book. However, the desserts require freshly made paneer. Homemade paneer certainly tastes better and does not take a lot of effort to make. I use whole milk but if you want you can add up to a quart of half and half for a richer taste. When the paneer is drained, the loose curds, called chenna, are used for desserts or in recipes such as Paneer Bhujri (page 145) and Kesar Bhapa Sandesh (page 223). The paneer can also be gathered and pressed to form blocks that can be cubed and used for recipes such as Saag Paneer (page 142).

MAKES	TOTAL TIME: 2 TO 3 HOURS	DIETARY
1½ cups	Prep and Drain Time: 2 to 3 hours Sauté Time: 10 minutes	

INGREDIENTS

1 gallon whole milk

6 tablespoons fresh lime or lemon juice

Colander and Cheesecloth for draining

INSTRUCTIONS

1. Pour the milk in the Instant Pot® and set it on Sauté mode. (Alternately, you can close the lid and select the Yogurt button to turn on the boil function. This takes a little longer.) Once the milk reaches a boil, about 10 minutes, press Cancel to turn off the Sauté mode.

2. Add 1 tablespoon of the lime or lemon juice at a time, stirring after each addition. Gradually the milk solids will separate from the whey. Carefully pour the mixture into a cheesecloth-lined colander.

3. When all the solids are gathered, let the cheesecloth hang to drain the whey. (Alternately, gather the solids into a round disc, place between two plates and place a weight over the top plate.) Let this drain for 2 to 3 hours. Remove the paneer from the cheesecloth and cut into cubes to use as needed. Paneer can be stored in the refrigerator for up to one week.

Basic Hardboiled Eggs

———

The Instant Pot® does a great job of boiling eggs in 5 minutes of pressure cooking, with the added benefit that it is very easy to peel eggs after they have been pressure cooked. I have often found it a lifesaver to have hardboiled eggs on hand. It is great to be able to transform them into a quick egg curry (see pages 189-193).

TOTAL TIME: 10 MINUTES
Pressure Cook: 4 minutes
Steam Release: 5 minutes

INSTRUCTIONS

Put 6 eggs in the Instant Pot® and pour in 1½ cups of water. Put on the lid and set the Instant Pot® on Manual Pressure for 4 minutes. Allow for Natural Pressure Release for 5 minutes and then do a Quick Release for any residual pressure. Store eggs in the refrigerator and use as needed.

Ghee

———

You can get pretty decent commercially made ghee (yes, I said that!). However, there is a satisfaction in making your own and it is done very quickly in the Instant Pot®. For best results use a dense organic European butter such as Kerrygold. The bonus is that this does work out to be much cheaper than commercially bought organic ghee.

TOTAL TIME: 15 MINUTES
Prep Time: 5 minutes
Sauté Time: 8 to 9 minutes

INSTRUCTIONS

1. Put 1 pound unsalted organic butter in the Instant Pot® and set it on the Sauté mode. Allow the butter to cook for 9 minutes, stirring once. Turn off the heat and let the butter stop boiling.

2. Strain the ghee through a cheesecloth into a small mason or other jar and seal and use as needed.

Everyday Masala Paste

Several Indian recipes start with this everyday curry paste (see index under "Everyday Masala Paste"). At its heart is a well-browned base of onion, ginger, and garlic. This process takes a good 10 minutes making it a little time consuming on a busy day. Making it in large quantities when time permits is like a gift to yourself for those busy days.

MAKES

1½ cups

TOTAL TIME: 45 MINUTES
Prep Time: 6 minutes
Sauté Time: 15 minutes / 5 minutes
Pressure Cook (Low): 4 minutes
Pressure Release: 15 minutes

DIETARY

INGREDIENTS

⅓ cup canola oil

1 tablespoon cumin seeds

2 cups chopped red onions

2 tablespoons minced fresh garlic (about 10 cloves)

2 tablespoons grated fresh ginger

1 tablespoon minced green chilies

4 pounds tomatoes, diced

1 tablespoon ground coriander

1 tablespoon ground cumin

1½ teaspoons salt (this is relatively low)

INSTRUCTIONS

1. Set the Instant Pot® on Sauté mode and pour in the oil. After about 3 minutes add the cumin seeds and cook until the seeds begin to sizzle.

2. Add the onions and cook for 3 to 4 minutes until they begin to wilt and soften. Stir in the garlic and ginger and cook for another 2 minutes. Stir in the chilies, tomatoes, coriander, cumin, and salt and cook for 5 minutes.

3. Press Cancel to turn off the Sauté mode, close the lid, and put on Manual Low Pressure setting for 4 minutes. When cooking time is complete, allow for Natural Pressure Release. This takes about 15 minutes.

4. Once the pressure is released, remove the lid and mix well to form an even base. Put the Instant Pot® on Sauté setting again and let the mixture thicken for about 5 minutes.

5. Cool and store in jars in the refrigerator for up to a week or freeze in ½ cup portions for longer storage (silicone egg molds work well for this).

Basic Makhani Masala

At the heart of many Indian dishes is this mild, rich-tasting sauce (see index under "Basic Makhani Masala"). My version uses coconut milk which keeps it vegan, allowing the recipe to be more versatile. I recommend using this make-ahead sauce to save time without compromising flavor for any Makhani-based recipes.

MAKES

4 cups

TOTAL TIME: 45 MINUTES
Prep Time: 5 minutes plus 5 to 10 minutes at end
Sauté Time: 15 minutes
Pressure Cook: 7 minutes
Pressure Release: about 10 minutes

DIETARY

INGREDIENTS

⅓ cup canola oil

1 tablespoon cumin seeds

1½ cups diced red onions

2 tablespoons minced fresh garlic

2 tablespoons grated fresh ginger

4 pounds tomatoes, diced, or 3 cups canned diced tomatoes

1 tablespoon garam masala (page 31 or storebought)

1 teaspoon cayenne pepper powder (more or less to taste)

1½ teaspoons salt

1 teaspoon sugar

1½ cups coconut milk

½ cup dried fenugreek leaves (kasuri methi)

INSTRUCTIONS

1. Set the Instant Pot® on Sauté mode and heat the oil. After about 3 minutes, add the cumin seeds and sauté until the seeds begin to sizzle. Add the onions and cook for 3 to 4 minutes, until they begin to wilt and soften. Add the garlic and ginger and cook for another 2 minutes. Stir in the tomatoes, garam masala, cayenne pepper powder, salt, and sugar, and cook for 5 minutes.

2. Press Cancel to turn off the Sauté mode, close the lid, and put on Manual Pressure mode for 7 minutes.

3. When cooking time is complete, allow for Natural Pressure Release for 5 minutes, then do a Quick Release for any residual pressure.

4. Open the lid and stir in the coconut milk. Using an immersion blender, puree the sauce until it is relatively smooth.

5. Stir in the fenugreek leaves, set the Instant Pot® on the Sauté mode, and heat through for 2 minutes.

6. Cool the sauce and store in the refrigerator for up to a week, or freeze in small containers and use as needed.

Garam Masala

Fragrant warm spices such as cloves, cinnamon, and cardamom come together in this all-purpose blend. Like practically everything in Indian cooking, there is no one recipe for garam masala—it varies from household to household, and consequently from chef to chef. For example, I do not add cumin to my garam masala mixture, but it is used in several variations of the spice blend. I have officially replaced certain other spice blends such as the pumpkin spice blend used in baking with my homemade garam masala blend. This spice blend is used in many of the recipes in this cookbook so it is a good one to make ahead and have on hand.

MAKES	TOTAL TIME: 10 MINUTES	DIETARY
¼ cup	Toast Time: 2 minutes Cool Time: 5 minutes Grinding Time: 3 minutes	

INGREDIENTS

⅓ cup green cardamom seeds

3 or 4 (2-inch) cinnamon sticks

2 or 3 dried bay leaves

1 or 2 star anise

¼ cup whole cloves

1 teaspoon black peppercorns

2 teaspoons cumin seeds (optional)

INSTRUCTIONS

1. Place all the ingredients in a dry skillet and lightly toast for about 1 to 2 minutes. Set aside to cool.

2. Grind the toasted spices in a spice mill or coffee grinder. Store in an airtight jar in a cool place.

Sambhar Masala

Sambhar Masala is a very versatile spice blend. It is essential for the South Indian stew called Sambhar (page 100) but I love using this for all coconut-based stews as well.

MAKES

1 cup

TOTAL TIME: 15 MINUTES
Toast Time: 6 minutes
Cool Time: 5 minutes
Grinding Time: 3 minutes

DIETARY

INGREDIENTS

½ cup coriander seeds

2 tablespoons cumin seeds

16 dried red chilies

1 tablespoon fenugreek seeds

1 tablespoon ground black pepper

2 tablespoons split Bengal gram lentils (chana dal)

1 tablespoon white urad dal

⅓ cup curry leaves

1 teaspoon black mustard seeds

½ tablespoon asafoetida

½ tablespoon ground turmeric

INSTRUCTIONS

1. Place all the ingredients in a cast iron skillet and toast for about 6 minutes. The spices should be fragrant and a few shades darker. Set aside to cool.

2. Place the toasted mixture in a spice mill or coffee grinder and grind until smooth. Store in an airtight jar.

Biryani Masala

This spice blend is a more aromatic variation of garam masala (page 31) and is used most frequently for layered rice dishes called biryani, such as my Awadi Gosht Biryani (page 76). This variation is my blend and I find it more flavorful than most of those found in supermarkets.

MAKES

½ cup

TOTAL TIME: 15 MINUTES
Toast Time: 5 minutes
Cool Time: 5 minutes
Grinding Time: 3 minutes

DIETARY

INGREDIENTS

1½ teaspoons cumin seeds

1½ teaspoons coriander seeds

½ teaspoon caraway seeds

2 dried red chilies

½ teaspoon green cardamom seeds

1 large cinnamon stick

2 star anise

2 dried bay leaves

¾ teaspoon whole cloves

¼ teaspoon black peppercorns

⅛ teaspoon ground nutmeg

INSTRUCTIONS

1. Place all the ingredients in a heavy-bottomed skillet and toast for 4 to 5 minutes. Set aside to cool.

2. Grind the toasted mixture to a powder in a spice mill or coffee grinder. Store in an airtight container in a cool dry place.

Tandoori Masala

I find this tandoori masala to be a very versatile, all-purpose spice blend. It is traditionally used as a rub for grilling or Tandoor-style cooking.

MAKES

⅓ cup

TOTAL TIME: 10 MINUTES
Toast Time: 2 minutes
Cool Time: 5 minutes
Grinding Time: 3 minutes

DIETARY

INGREDIENTS

3 tablespoons coriander seeds

3 tablespoons cumin seeds

4 dried red chilies (optional)

1 teaspoon carom seeds (ajwain)

2 or 3 (2-inch) cinnamon sticks

10 whole cloves

1½ teaspoons cardamom seeds

2 tablespoons Kashmiri red chili powder

INSTRUCTIONS

1. Place the coriander seeds, cumin seeds, dried red chilies, carom seeds, cinnamon sticks, cloves, and cardamom seeds in a skillet and toast for 2 minutes, until fragrant. Set aside to cool.

2. Grind the toasted mixture to a powder in a spice mill or coffee grinder. Stir in the red chili powder.

3. Store in an airtight jar and use as needed.

Fresh Ginger Garlic Paste

MAKES

⅓ cup

TOTAL TIME: 5 MINUTES

DIETARY

INGREDIENTS

1 large piece (about ¼ pound) ginger, peeled and coarsely chopped

20 cloves garlic

3 green chilies

⅓ cup chopped cilantro

4 tablespoons freshly squeezed lime juice

1 teaspoon salt

INSTRUCTIONS

1. Place all ingredients in a blender and process until smooth.

2. Store in a jar in the refrigerator for up to a couple of weeks or freeze in small containers and use as needed.

How to Sprout your Beans in the Instant Pot®

Take your favorite beans, such as whole moong beans or adzuki beans, and soak in water for 6 to 8 hours. Place the soaked beans in the Instant Pot® with about 3 tablespoons of water, close the lid, and turn on the Yogurt setting which will automatically set for 8 hours. You should begin to see sprouts after this time, though I have seen some stubborn beans that actually need 12 hours to get started.

No-Knead Naan

I could not close this chapter out without giving you an amazing but ridiculously simple recipe for naan to sop up the wonderful succulent curries in this book. You just can't go wrong with naan—it combines the comfort of fresh baked bread with a uniquely Indian twist. Though it is difficult to replicate the effect of the tandoor or traditional clay oven in which naan is typically cooked, this recipe gets you close using just a cast iron skillet. The best part of this recipe is how quickly and perfectly the naan dough ferments in the Instant Pot®.

MAKES	TOTAL TIME: 2 HOURS	DIETARY
8 naans	Prep Time: 15 minutes Yogurt Setting: 1 hour Cook Time: 40 minutes	

INGREDIENTS

4 tablespoons oil

¼ cup whole milk

1 teaspoon sugar

1 tablespoon rapid-rise yeast

3½ cups all-purpose flour, plus more for rolling

2 teaspoons salt

½ cup plain whole-milk yogurt

1 egg, beaten

Nigella seeds and butter for finishing

INSTRUCTIONS

1. Set the Instant Pot® on Sauté mode and allow to heat for about 1 minute and then press Cancel.

2. Pour in the oil and then the milk. (The warmth of the Instant Pot® will get the milk to the right temperature to quickly proof the yeast.) Stir in the sugar and then the yeast. The mixture should become frothy within a minute or so.

3. Gradually stir in the flour and salt with a wooden spoon. The mixture will become crumbly. Stir in the yogurt and egg—this should be enough moisture to make a soft dough. Use your hands to press it all together into a ball (the objective is to have a soft smooth dough).

4. Cover the Instant Pot®, and set it on the Yogurt setting for 60 minutes.

5. Open the Instant Pot® to see beautifully risen soft and fluffy dough. Remove the dough and place on a

working surface. Mix in a little extra flour if you feel the dough is too sticky. Break the dough into 8 lemon-size balls and roll each to an oval about 5 to 6 inches in length and about ⅛ inch in thickness (the naans should be rolled out fairly thin as this allows them to puff up while cooking; you can use extra flour for rolling, but shake off any excess flour after rolling).

6. Heat a cast iron griddle for at least 2 to 3 minutes (test with water to ensure heat). Place one dough oval in the griddle. After a couple of minutes, it should puff a little at spots. Quickly turn on the other side and sprinkle with a few nigella seeds. Press the seeds gently to set into the dough. Cook for a couple of more minutes—the bread should be puffy and well browned and lightly charred at spots. Repeat with remaining dough disks. If desired, drizzle with a little butter before serving.

BREAKFAST & SNACKS

The Indian breakfast is an interesting, well-kept secret. Whole grains and cereals are tossed together with light seasonings to create a variety of flavorful, filling dishes that we like to call *upmas*. Indian brunch fare will evoke nostalgic memories for anyone who has grown up with it. It is what my heart craves on weekend mornings. And on busy weekend mornings, with the delayed start and other fix-and-forget options, the Instant Pot® has ended up being a game changer. It is wonderful to be able to conveniently bring back to our breakfast table a repertoire of dishes that are nutritious, amazingly flavorful, and deeply rooted in the Indian Ayurveda tradition of cooking.

From the Udupi region of southern India, we get a collection of snack offerings known collectively as "tiffin." The base of several of these much-loved dishes, for instance *idlis* and *dosas*, is a classic batter of fermented rice and lentils. The process of fermentation boosts the nutritional value of the grains and makes them easy to digest. And the best part is that the Instant Pot® makes fermenting the batter a cinch. My son happens to be very fond of his *dosas*, and thanks to perfect 8-hour fermentation of the batter in the Instant Pot®, I can become Super Mom and serve them often without having to worry about the super chilly elements of the New York winter when fermenting the batter even indoors is tricky. As for steaming items like *idlis*, it has taken me years and years of using multiple crazy devices to finally find something that magically steams as if a genie granted my wish. Many times I have sighed and said, "Instant Pot®, where have you been all my life?"

What *tiffin* is to southern India, *farsan* is to western India, and *jhalkhabar* is to eastern India. The most popular *farsan* is the Gujarati assortment of steamed wholegrain cakes called *dhoklas*—I have culled and tested out one of my favorite recipes for you (page 50). These snacks can serve double duty on your dinner table as a side dish. In the north there are similar medleys, but sprouts and legumes are king, and why not? Sprouting legumes boosts their nutritional value to that of a superfood, and also makes them much simpler to digest. Interestingly enough, you can sprout chickpeas or adzuki beans before cooking them in curries in the Instant Pot®! (See page 35.) It takes a little upfront investment of time, but you will reap many nutritional rewards.

So stock your pantry with a few essential grains and legumes, and start your day with fun, traditional light meals from all around India.

Essential Dosa/Idli/Oothapam Batter

This batter forms the base of the next few recipes: Idlis (pages 43), Kanjipuran Idlis (page 45), Oothapams (page 46), Masala Dosas (page 47). The basic batter is used for a multitude of snack dishes known as "tiffin" in South Indian parlance. I offer two examples in this book to assist you with fueling your imagination. The process of fermentation is made foolproof and manageable by using the yogurt setting of the Instant Pot®. All said and done, making idlis or dosas does need a little planning, but once made, the batter keeps well in the refrigerator for up to a week.

MAKES

1 batch

TOTAL TIME: 14½ HOURS
Soak Time: 6 hours
Prep Time: 20 minutes
Yogurt Mode: 8 hours

DIETARY

INGREDIENTS

¾ cup white split lentils (white urad dal)

2 cups idli rice or other parboiled rice *(do not use basmati rice)*

½ teaspoon fenugreek seeds

2 teaspoons salt

INSTRUCTIONS

1. Place the urad dal in a bowl and add 2 cups of water. Place the rice, fenugreek seeds, and salt in a separate bowl and add 2 cups of water. Let both soak for at least 6 hours.

2. In either a stone grinder or a blender, first blend the urad dal with very little water until light and fluffy. Remove and set in a large container or in the steel cooking pot insert of the Instant Pot®.

3. Put the rice mixture in the blender and blend until smooth with just a hint of texture. Mix with the lentil mixture. You can use your hands to mix, as bacteria from your hands actually assists with fermentation.

4. Place the mixture in your Instant Pot®, close the lid, and set the Instant Pot® to Yogurt setting. Let it ferment for 8 hours. Open the lid to be greeted with well-fermented batter. (If you are not going to use the batter right away, you can store it in the refrigerator for up to a week.)

Idlis

Soft Steamed Rice and Lentil Cakes

An idli is a steamed, soft cakelike savory bun, made with a naturally gluten-free sourdough batter of rice and lentils. This is a relatively light and nourishing offering from South India. Idlis are steamed in special molds easily available online (they are sold in multi-layered stands). However, in the event you cannot procure an idli mold/stand, you can actually steam these as a large cake in an 8-inch round cake pan much like the Dhokla (page 50), and cut it into wedges.

SERVES

4 to 6

TOTAL TIME: 25 MINUTES plus 14 hours for
making batter
Steam Time (Low): 8 minutes
Pressure Release: 15 minutes

DIETARY

INGREDIENTS

1 batch Essential Dosa/Idli/
Oothapam batter (page 41)

Idli molds/stand *(can be found
online)*

INSTRUCTIONS

1. Grease the idli molds with oil and pour the batter into the molds until about three-quarters filled.

2. Fill the Instant Pot® with about 1½ cups of water. Place the idli stand in the Instant Pot®. Close the lid and set on Steam mode on low for about 8 minutes.

3. Allow for Natural Pressure Release for about 15 minutes. Remove idlis and serve hot. Serve idlis with Tomato Onion Chutney (page 233), Milagu Podi (page 240), and if desired with Sambhar (page 100).

Kanjipuram Idlis
Well-Seasoned Masala Rice and Lentil Cakes

Rumor has it that Kanjipuram idlis were first made in the Varadharaja Perumal temple in Kanchipuram in Southern India. In this temple, idlis are actually made in a conical shape. For most household and everyday variations, this idli is made in the regular idli mold, but with the masala tempering.

SERVES	TOTAL TIME: 30 MINUTES plus 14 hours for making batter	DIETARY
4 to 6	Sauté Time: 5 minutes Steam Time: 8 minutes Pressure Release: 15 minutes	

INGREDIENTS

1 tablespoon oil

1 teaspoon mustard seeds

1 tablespoon grated fresh ginger

1 tablespoon split Bengal gram lentils (chana dal)

1 teaspoon white split lentils (white urad dal)

1 teaspoon freshly ground black pepper

2 tablespoons chopped cilantro

1 batch Essential Dosa/Idli/ Oothapam Batter (page 41)

Idli molds/stand (can be found online)

INSTRUCTIONS

1. Heat the oil in a small skillet on the stovetop and add the mustard seeds and cook until they begin to crackle. Stir in the ginger and both lentils/dals. Mix in the black pepper. Remove from heat and stir in the cilantro. Add this mixture to the prepared idli batter.

2. Grease the idli molds with oil and pour the batter into the molds until about three-quarters filled.

3. Fill the Instant Pot® with about 1½ cups water. Place the idli stand in the Instant Pot®. Close the lid and set on Steam mode for about 8 minutes.

4. Allow for Natural Pressure Release for about 15 minutes. Remove idlis and serve hot.

Oothapams
Savory Rice and Lentil Pancakes

These pancakes are made with dosa batter, usually after the batter has aged a little to allow room for it to ferment and get fairly sour. For oothapams, I sometimes like to substitute half or all the dosa batter with a mixture of brown rice and regular rice, or even brown rice and quinoa. I have found that this substitution works especially well for these oothapams and the dosas. It is best to have a cast iron griddle for cooking these, I use a standard one from Lodge that I have now had for several years. It is put to use every weekend and is no worse for the wear.

SERVES	TOTAL TIME: 25 MINUTES plus 14 hours for making batter	DIETARY
4 to 6	Prep Time: 10 minutes Cook Time: 10 minutes	

INGREDIENTS

1 batch Essential Dosa/Idli/ Oothapam Batter (page 41)

Canola or grapeseed oil for tempering

½ cup green peas

1 medium onion, chopped

1 medium carrot, chopped

2 green chilies, minced

Chopped cilantro

INSTRUCTIONS

1. Heat a cast iron griddle. To test for heat, add a few drops of water, the water should dance off the surface, form beads, and then evaporate.

2. Gently add a little oil and pour one or two ladlefuls of the batter in two corners of the griddle. They should be about 4 inches in diameter and have the depth of a pancake. Scatter some of the peas, onion, carrot, and green chilies over the batter. This allows the vegetables to cook as the batter sets. Cook on medium-low heat until the pancake sets, about 2 to 3 minutes—it is good to cover the pan to allow for even and quick cooking.

3. With a spatula carefully loosen the pancake, turn, and cook on the other side for just 1 minute—you do not want to burn the vegetables. Remove and keep warm while making additional oothapams.

4. Serve hot with Tomato Onion Chutney (page 233) or Coconut Chutney (page 232).

Masala Dosas
Rice and Lentil Crepes with Spinach and Cheese

The third classic item that can be made with versatile fermented rice and lentil batter, along with Idlis (page 43) and Oothapams (page 46), are dosas. These are thin, crisp lentil crepes, usually served with a potato filling. To balance the protein I have used a spinach and paneer filling. I start the fermentation process for the batter and once the batter is ready, I start the potatoes while I make the crepes. While these dosas are certainly a great Sunday brunch item, they are also a tasty dinner item if you want to mix and match the fillings. The scrambled Paneer Bhujri recipe (page 145) also makes a great filling. A good cast iron griddle is best for making dosas.

MAKES	TOTAL TIME: 25 MINUTES plus 14 hours for making batter	DIETARY
6 crepes	Prep Time: 5 minutes Cook Time: 20 minutes	

INGREDIENTS

1 batch Essential Dosa/Idli/Oothapam Batter (page 41)

1 large onion, halved (for cleaning the griddle)

1 cup crumbled fresh paneer (page 26)

½ cup grated cheddar cheese

1 cup baby spinach leaves

INSTRUCTIONS

1. Heat the griddle on the stovetop. Test with a drop of water, if it sizzles and dances off the surface of the griddle it is hot enough. Turn the heat to medium-low and add a little oil around the griddle, this will be needed just for the first dosa.

2. Pour about ⅓ cup of the batter on the griddle and spread outward with the back of the spoon to form a 6- to 8-inch thin crepe. While the crepe is cooking add a little crumbled paneer, cheese and some spinach leaves on one half of the dosa. Allow the cheese to melt. Let this cook for 2 minutes or until the crepe comes off the surface easily and is crisp and golden brown. Fold the crepe over and remove from the pan.

3. Repeat with the remaining batter and cheese to make a total of 6 crepes.

Daliya Upma
Cracked Wheat Breakfast Pilaf

This cracked wheat pilaf is an easy and nourishing way to start the morning. It offers minerals, proteins, and a good dose of vegetables to get you going. This wholesome dish was often made in the early morning hours in my mother-in-law's kitchen. Breakfast or nashta is a big deal in North Indian homes, and this is adapted from our family recipe. If you want a gluten-free variation, you can use coarse polenta in place of the wheat for this dish.

SERVES

4 to 6

TOTAL TIME: 15 MINUTES
Prep Time: 10 minutes
Sauté Time: 3 minutes
Pressure Cook: 2 minutes

DIETARY

INGREDIENTS

2 tablespoons oil

1 teaspoon black mustard seeds

1 tablespoon grated fresh ginger

1 medium red onion, minced

10 to 12 fresh curry leaves

2 or 3 dried red chilies, broken into 2 or 3 pieces

1 red potato, chopped (skin on)

1 cup assorted mixed fresh vegetables, chopped (I use a carrot, ear of corn, and handful of green beans)

½ cup coarse bulgur or cracked wheat

1 teaspoon salt

½ teaspoon garam masala (optional)

¼ cup frozen green peas (unthawed)

2 tablespoons chopped cilantro

2 tablespoons fresh lime juice

INSTRUCTIONS

1. Set the Instant Pot® on Sauté mode and heat the oil. Add the mustard seeds and wait until the seeds crackle. Add the ginger and red onion and sauté until soft and translucent.

2. Add the curry leaves and dried red chilies and mix well. Add the potato, vegetables, cracked wheat, and salt and stir well. Stir in the garam masala (if using) and 1 cup of water.

3. Press Cancel to turn off the Sauté mode. Cover the pot and set on Manual Pressure mode for 2 minutes.

4. When cooking time is complete, use Quick Pressure Release.

5. Remove the lid and add the frozen peas. Stir in the cilantro and lime juice and let it rest for a few minutes before serving.

Khaman Dhokla
Steamed Savory Chickpea Flour Cakes

A dhokla is a savory cake, a signature dish from the western state of Gujarat. The traditional version uses a mixture of rice and lentils that are soaked, ground, and then fermented. The variation given here is often referred to as an instant version as the mixture uses chickpea flour (besan) and fruit salts for creating the leavening effect. To make this dish I use Eno fruit salts, available at Indian grocery stores and many online sights. If you cannot find Eno, a combination of baking soda and baking powder should work.

SERVES	TOTAL TIME: 40 MINUTES	DIETARY
4 to 6	Prep Time: 10 minutes Steam Time (without pressure): 15 minutes Rest Time: 10 minutes Tempering Time: 3 minutes	

INGREDIENTS

For dhokla:

1¼ cups chickpea flour (besan)

1 tablespoons fine semolina or polenta

½ teaspoon ground turmeric

½ teaspoon cayenne pepper powder

1 teaspoon grated fresh ginger

1 green chili

1 teaspoon sugar

1 teaspoon salt

⅓ cup plain or coconut yogurt (commercial or see recipe page 24)

1 tablespoon fresh lime juice

1 tablespoon Eno fruit salt

INSTRUCTIONS

Make dhokla:

1. Generously grease an 8-inch round cake pan with oil and set aside.

2. Put the chickpea flour, semolina, turmeric, and cayenne pepper powder in a mixing bowl and mix well with a whisk to remove any lumps—this is very important.

3. Place the ginger, green chili, sugar, salt, and ¼ cup of water in a blender and blend until smooth. Add the mixture to the chickpea flour mixture. Add the yogurt and lime juice and beat until smooth—you should have the texture of a loose and light cake batter. The beating allows you to incorporate air and gives the cake the lightness that it needs.

4. Place about 2 cups of water in the Instant Pot® and place the trivet in the pot. Set the Instant Pot® on Sauté

For tempering:

1 tablespoon oil

1 teaspoon black mustard seeds

1 teaspoon sesame seeds

1 tablespoon coconut flakes

1 or 2 whole dried red chilies

1/8 teaspoon asafoetida powder

10 curry leaves

1 teaspoon salt

1/2 teaspoon sugar

2 tablespoons fresh lime juice

2 tablespoons chopped cilantro

mode (this will allow the steaming process to start sooner resulting in a lighter dhokla). Working quickly, add the fruit salt to the batter and stir lightly—the batter should become frothy and light. Immediately pour the batter into the greased cake pan and place the pan on the trivet. Cover with a piece of foil. Close the lid, and press Cancel to turn off Sauté mode. Set the Instant Pot® on Steam mode for 15 minutes with the vent open (if you have an Ultra Instant Pot®, steam using no pressure).

5. When the cooking time is complete, allow to rest for 10 minutes.

6. Open the lid and remove the cake pan from the Instant Pot®. Remove the foil, loosen the edges of the dhokla with a knife and then invert the dhokla onto a plate.

Tempering:

7. Heat the oil in a small pan. Add the mustard seeds, sesame seeds, coconut flakes, dried chilies, asafoetida powder, and curry leaves. When the mustard seeds begin to crackle turn off the heat and lightly stir in the salt, sugar, lime juice and 1/4 cup of water.

8. Pour this seasoned liquid evenly over the inverted dhokla, allowing it to absorb the liquid. Sprinkle with the cilantro, cut into wedges, and serve.

Sevai Upma
Stir-Fried Indian Vermicelli with Vegetables

Sevai Upma or Vermicelli Upma is a breakfast dish that is super easy to put together. This is a very basic version that I sometimes even make with frozen mixed vegetables. Quick breakfast dishes like this are popular all across India, and the seasoning varies depending on the region. This particular variation is the way I make it in my household. Thin Indian rice (if you want to keep this gluten-free) or wheat vermicelli works best for this recipe. If you wish you can use angel hair pasta, broken up, too.

SERVES	TOTAL TIME: 20 MINUTES	DIETARY
4 to 6	Prep Time: 5 minutes Sauté Time: 4 minutes Pressure Cook (Low): 1 minute Pressure Release: 5 minutes	

INGREDIENTS

1 tablespoon canola or grapeseed oil

1 teaspoon mustard seeds

1 medium onion, thinly sliced

1½ cups thin vermicelli (about 8 ounces), broken into pieces if long strands

1 tomato, chopped

1 red or green bell pepper, sliced

1 cup frozen peas

1 carrot, minced

1 teaspoon salt, or to taste

1 teaspoon cayenne pepper powder, or to taste

2 to 3 tablespoons fresh lime juice

1 tablespoon chopped cilantro

INSTRUCTIONS

1. Set the Instant Pot® to Sauté mode, and heat the oil. Add the mustard seeds and onion and sauté for about 3 minutes.

2. Stir in the vermicelli, tomato, bell pepper, frozen peas, carrot, salt, cayenne pepper powder, and ½ cup of water.

3. Press Cancel to turn off the Sauté mode, close the lid, and set on Manual Low Pressure mode for 1 minute.

4. When cooking time is complete, allow for Natural Pressure Release for 5 minutes and then use Quick Release to vent the remaining steam.

5. Stir the vermicelli well. Stir in the lime juice and cilantro and serve.

Pongal

Rice and Lentil Porridge with Pepper and Cashews

This comforting porridge-like dish, from the Tamil Nadu region of India, is similar in concept to Chinese congee. The porridge setting of the Instant Pot® works wonders with this dish. My children learn Bharatnatyam, classical South Indian dance. Last year they had their arangetram or stage debut. We hosted a trio of very talented musicians from India who were their orchestra. I perfected this recipe with their critiquing. The Instant Pot® made it very easy to make multiple variations. And my secret guilt-free ingredient is quinoa.

SERVES	**TOTAL TIME: 35 MINUTES**	**DIETARY**
4 to 6	Prep Time: 6 minutes Saute Time: 4 minutes Porridge Mode: 15 minutes Pressure Release: 10 minutes	

INGREDIENTS

2 tablespoons ghee (page 27)

¼ cup cashews

1 teaspoon black mustard seeds

1 tablespoon cracked black peppercorns

1 or 2 whole dried red chilies

10 to 12 curry leaves

½ cup rice

¾ cup quinoa

¾ cup yellow split lentils (moong dal)

1 tablespoon grated fresh ginger

1 teaspoon cayenne pepper powder

1 teaspoon salt, or to taste

Chopped cilantro (optional)

INSTRUCTIONS

1. Set the Instant Pot to Sauté mode. Heat 1 teaspoon of the ghee. Add the cashews and gently stir until they are pale brown. Remove with a slotted spoon.

2. Add the remaining ghee to the Instant Pot and heat for about 45 seconds. Add the mustard seeds and wait until they begin to crackle. Add the peppercorns, chilies, and curry leaves. Press Cancel to turn off the Sauté mode.

3. Add the rice, quinoa, and lentils to the Instant Pot®. Add 2 cups of water, the ginger, cayenne pepper powder, and salt. Close the lid and set on Porridge mode for 15 minutes.

4. When the cooking time is complete, allow for a Natural Pressure Release for at least 10 minutes. Once pressure is released, open the lid and stir well (the consistency should be thick).

5. Stir in the cashew nuts and garnish with the cilantro, if using, before serving.

Misal Chauli Chaat
Sprouted Bean Salad

———

Sprouted legumes are a very nutritious creation and a popular breakfast in various parts of India. This recipe is done like a chaat or North Indian salad. My children find the idea of legumes with little tails rather amusing. Sprouting the legumes does require some planning ahead but not really a lot of effort with your Instant Pot®. This can be enjoyed at breakfast or along with a meal as a salad.

SERVES

4 to 6

TOTAL TIME: 30 MINUTES (plus about 16 to 18 hours to sprout the beans)
Prep Time: 5 minutes
Pressure Cook: 2 minutes
Steam Release: 10 minutes
Resting Time: 10 minutes

DIETARY

INGREDIENTS

1½ cups sprouted moong or adzuki beans (see instructions on page 35)

2 medium potatoes, peeled and cubed (about 1 cup)

1½ teaspoons salt

½ teaspoon ground turmeric

1 medium red onion, chopped

2 teaspoons chaat masala

½ cup pomegranate seeds

2 tablespoons fresh lime juice

½ cup coarsely crushed toasted peanuts

2 tablespoons chopped cilantro

INSTRUCTIONS

1. Place the sprouted beans and potatoes in the Instant Pot®. Stir in ½ teaspoon of the salt, the turmeric, and 2 cups of water. Close the lid and set on Pressure Cook mode for 2 minutes.

2. When cooking time is complete, allow for Natural Pressure Release for 5 minutes, then use Quick Release for any residual pressure. Open the lid. The potatoes should be soft and beans somewhat crunchy.

3. Drain the mixture and place in a mixing bowl. Add the remaining 1 teaspoon salt, the red onion, chaat masala, pomegranate seeds, and lime juice and mix well. Stir in the toasted peanuts and chopped cilantro. Allow the flavors to sit and blend for 10 minutes before serving.

Tamatar Masala Anda
Poached Eggs in Tomato Sauce

These eggs are an Anglo-Indian creation, probably an Indian version of shakshuka. *I love to make them when I have made a fresh batch of Everyday Masala Paste—after all, more than half the work is done that way! They make a great hearty breakfast or a light meal. The eggs in this dish are soft rather than runny and taste indulgently creamy. My son refers to this dish as his special eggs.*

SERVES

4

TOTAL TIME: 15 MINUTES (plus 40 minutes to make Everyday Masala Paste if needed)
Prep Time: 3 minutes
Sauté Time: 10 minutes

DIETARY

INGREDIENTS

1 cup Everyday Masala Paste (page 29)

½ cup coconut milk

½ teaspoon red pepper flakes

4 eggs

1 tablespoon chopped cilantro

INSTRUCTIONS

1. Set the Instant Pot® on Sauté mode. Add the Everyday Masala Paste and cook for 3 to 4 minutes, until the masala cooks down some—this helps the onions in the masala paste caramelize and imparts a deep rich taste to the sauce.

2. Add the coconut milk and stir well. Bring to a simmer. Sprinkle with the red pepper flakes.

3. Carefully crack the eggs over the tomato sauce in four separate spots. Close the lid and set to cook for 2 minutes still on Sauté mode. (When ready the egg yolks should be gently set and slightly runny if poked; they will develop a soft skin on top.) Sprinkle with chopped cilantro. To serve gently lift out each egg and some sauce with a large spoon and place on plate.

RICE & NOODLES

Rice, grains, or flatbreads are usually at the center of the Indian plate. There are about as many varieties of rice in India as there are regional dimensions for Indian cooking. To keep things simple, the recipes here use the classic and brown varieties of basmati rice. The Instant Pot® has helped me discover brown rice again. The rice setting does a magical job of cooking brown rice to a perfect, slightly chewy texture. For everyday cooking, I converted two classic white rice dishes, Chingri Biryani (Shrimp and Rice Casserole; page 72) and Jeera Pulao (Cumin-Scented Rice; page 66), into brown rice dishes.

Festive or complex rice dishes usually fall into *pulaos* (pilafs), which can be lightly seasoned dishes, or more complex and layered dishes called *biryanis*. The biryani has many avatars depending on where in India it hails from. I have tried to showcase the two main styles, a North Indian biryani, which is the Awadhi Gosht Biryani (Layered Lamb and Rice Casserole; page 76) from the princely state of Awadh, and a South Indian chicken biryani, which is the Chettinaad Kozhi Biryani (page 80) from the Chettinad region of India. Other dishes, such as Yogurt Rice (page 67) and Khichuri (Bengali Red Lentil Risotto; page 74), are also signature dishes from different parts of the country. I am particularly fond of these one-pot rice dishes and feel that the Instant Pot® does an incredible job of maximizing their flavors.

When cooking rice in the Instant Pot®, it is important to allow time for a Natural Pressure Release. This ensures that the rice will bloom and fluff out to perfection. The Instant Pot® instruction and recipe guides that come with the appliance are good references for cooking rice. I embellished the rice guide a little to offer you Instant Pot® directions for the key rice varieties such as rosemata, ponni, basmati, and kalajeera. Much as we love our festive pulaos and biryanis, most everyday meals are served with plain rice. To cover every variety of popular rice eaten in India could be its own cookbook. Most recipes in this cookbook have been developed using basmati rice, but The Essential Instant Indian Rice Guide (next page) will allow you to mix and match if you truly enjoy another variety of rice.

The Essential *INSTANT* INDIAN **Rice Guide**

The basic process of cooking rice in the Instant Pot® involves rice, water, and turning on the Rice or Multigrain mode. In about twenty minutes, you will have the perfect rice of your choice. At the heart of cooking rice is knowing your water proportion. This guide will help. Here are six essential Indian rice varieties, demystified for cooking in the Instant Pot®.

BASMATI RICE

This rice is the most popular variety in India and is often mistaken for the only variety of rice found there. Grown in the foothills of the Himalayas in Northern India, it certainly is a workhorse rice and great for plain or festive dishes. It cooks up very well in the Instant Pot®.

1 cup basmati rice : 1¼ cups water
Rice mode with Natural Pressure Release
or
Manual Low Pressure for 12 minutes with Natural Pressure Release

BROWN BASMATI RICE

This variety is a somewhat guilt-free alternative to your delicate white basmati. I think I have managed to nail this down with Instant Pot®.

1 cup brown basmati rice : 1½ cups water
Multigrain mode for 15 minutes with Natural Pressure Release

PONNI RICE

This rice is mostly cultivated along the banks of the Kaveri River in the cities of Ariyalur, Trichy, and Madurai. It is a hybrid variety that is very popular in the southern parts of India. In fact, the name Ponni is a local name for the Kaveri.

1 cup rice : 1¼ cups water
Rice mode with Natural Pressure Release

ROSEMATA RICE

This pink partially husked and mildly sweet-tasting rice is a signature offering from the southern state of Kerala. It pairs well with any of the fish dishes in this book or is just as good with a hot, nourishing side of sambhar. This rice needs a lot of water and takes a little more time to cook than other varieties. I have found the Multigrain mode works well for this.

1 cup rosemata rice : 3 cups water
Multigrain mode for 15 minutes with Natural Pressure Release

SURTI KOLAM RICE

This is the comfort rice of Gujarat and western India. It is a neutral and fuss-free variety without any of the aroma of basmati. It is, however, a very soft and soothing rice and goes especially well with lentil and vegetable dishes.

1 cup rice : 1¼ cups water
Rice mode with Natural Pressure Release

GOVINDA BHOG or KALAJEERA RICE:

Govinda bhog is a much-loved signature rice from the eastern state of West Bengal. It is a short-grain, highly aromatic, and delicate rice, worth trying for a special festive meal. You can use it for recipes such as Misthi Pulao (page 79) and Khichuri (page 74).

1 cup rice : 1¼ cups water
Rice mode with 5 minutes Natural Pressure Release followed by Quick Pressure Release

Parsee Brown Rice
Caramelized Rice Pilaf with Fragrant Spices

This festive rice dish from the Parsee community of western India is an almost mandatory accompaniment to meat curries like Gosht Dhansak (page 202) and fish dishes like Patra ni Macchi (page 150). The gentle brown color is from the caramelized onions.

SERVES	TOTAL TIME: 40 MINUTES	DIETARY
4 to 6	Prep Time: 2 minutes Sauté Time: 11 minutes Rice Mode: 12 minutes Pressure Release: 15 minutes	

INGREDIENTS

2 tablespoon canola or grapeseed oil

1 large red onion, thinly sliced

1 teaspoon brown sugar

2 black cardamom pods

4 green cardamom pods

1 large (about 3 inches) cinnamon stick

1 or 2 dried bay leaves

4 cloves

2 blades mace

1 teaspoon salt, or to taste

1 cup basmati rice, rinsed and drained

INSTRUCTIONS

1. Set the Instant Pot® on Sauté mode, and heat the oil for 1 to 2 minutes.

2. Add the onion and gently cook for 3 minutes. When the onion wilts and softens, stir in the brown sugar and cook for 4 to 5 more minutes until the onion is softly caramelized.

3. Add the cardamom pods, cinnamon stick, bay leaves, cloves, mace, salt, and rice and stir and cook for another 2 minutes. Stir in 1¼ cups of water.

4. Press Cancel to turn off the Sauté mode, close the lid, and set the Instant Pot® on the Rice mode (12 minutes).

5. When cooking time is complete, allow for Natural Pressure Release for 10 to 15 minutes and then use Quick Release for any remaining pressure. Serve as an accompaniment with any dish.

Jeera Pulao
Cumin-Scented Brown Rice with Green Peas

One of my many delights with the Instant Pot® is how well it cooks brown rice and other complex grains. This cumin-scented rice is a makeover of a very basic rice pilaf often found on North Indian tables. It is complex enough to distinguish itself from basic white rice, but still easy to prepare for everyday meals.

SERVES

4 to 6

TOTAL TIME: 35 MINUTES
Prep Time: 2 minutes
Sauté Time: 3 minutes
Pressure Cook: 12 minutes
Pressure Release: 15 minutes

DIETARY

INGREDIENTS

1 tablespoon canola or grapeseed oil

1 teaspoon whole cumin seeds

1 or 2 bay leaves

1 teaspoon salt, or to taste

1 cup brown basmati rice

1 cup green peas (can be frozen)

INSTRUCTIONS

1. Set the Instant Pot® to Sauté mode, and heat the oil for 1 to 2 minutes.

2. Add the cumin seeds and bay leaves and heat until the cumin seeds begin to crackle. Stir in the salt and rice and about 1½ cups of water. Add the peas.

3. Press Cancel to turn off Sauté mode, close the lid, and set the Instant Pot® at the Manual Pressure setting for 12 minutes.

4. When cooking time is complete, allow at least 15 minutes for Natural Pressure Release, then use Quick Release for any residual pressure. Serve as an accompaniment to any other dish.

Tayir Shadum
Yogurt Rice

The classic ending to a south Indian meal is usually Tayir Shadum and South Indian pickle. This yogurt rice is considered essential for auspicious occasions. It is also a great way to use up leftover rice.

SERVES

4 to 6

TOTAL TIME: 15 MINUTES
Prep Time: 3 minutes
Pressure Cook: 7 minutes
Tempering Time: 2 minutes

DIETARY

INGREDIENTS

1 cup white basmati or other rice

1 cup milk

1 teaspoon salt

3 cups plain yogurt

For tempering:

1 tablespoon oil

1 teaspoon black mustard seeds

3 or 4 whole dried red chilies

10 to 12 curry leaves

2 tablespoon pomegranate seeds (optional)

INSTRUCTIONS

1. Place the rice and 2 cups of water in the Instant Pot®. Close the lid, and put on Manual Pressure setting for 7 minutes.

2. When cooking time is complete, do a Quick Release for the pressure. Open the lid, add the milk and stir into the rice.

3. In a separate bowl, beat the yogurt with the salt. Add yogurt mixture to the rice and mix well. Put rice in a serving dish.

4. Heat the oil in a small skillet and add the black mustard seeds. When the seeds crackle, stir in the red chilies and curry leaves. Cook for 1 to 2 minutes, then pour the oil mixture over the rice. Garnish with the pomegranate seeds (if using) and serve.

Kofta Pulao

Golden Rice Pilaf with Chicken Meatballs

From Lucknow in Uttar Pradesh, this Kofta Pulao is a festive rice with chicken meatballs, delicately seasoned with saffron and mint. It is elegant but much easier to put together than a more elaborate and formal biryani. Of course, as with most recipes, the Instant Pot® makes it even more manageable. The heat or chili quotient is a variable in this dish, and if you wish you can make the meatballs spicier.

SERVES	TOTAL TIME: 50 MINUTES	DIETARY
4 to 6	Prep Time: 10 minutes Sauté Time: 12 minutes Rice Mode: 12 minutes Pressure Release: 15 minutes	

INGREDIENTS

For meatballs:

1 pound ground chicken

2 tablespoons grated fresh ginger

1 tablespoon minced garlic

2 teaspoons ground cumin

1 teaspoon ground coriander

2 to 3 green chilies, minced

1½ teaspoons salt, or to taste

2 tablespoons lemon juice

1 egg, beaten

1 tablespoon cornstarch

INSTRUCTIONS

Make meatballs:

1. Place the ground chicken, ginger, garlic, cumin, coriander, green chilies, and salt in a bowl and mix together. Add the lemon juice, beaten egg, and cornstarch. Shape into walnut-size balls. (If you wish you can do this up to a day ahead as this enhances the flavors of the chicken.)

Prepare pilaf:

2. Set the Instant Pot® to Sauté mode and heat the ghee and oil. When the ghee is melted, add the onion and sauté for about 6 minutes, until the onion softens, wilts, and turns pale golden.

For the pilaf:

1 tablespoon ghee (page 27)

1 tablespoon canola or grapeseed oil

1 large onion, thinly sliced

1 cup basmati rice, rinsed and drained

½ cup chopped fresh mint

1 teaspoon salt, or to taste

1 teaspoon saffron strands

1 cinnamon stick (about 2 inches)

2 to 3 dried bay leaves

3. Gently add the meatballs and let them cook for at least 2 minutes. Take care not to stir until after 2 minutes, then turn them once and cook for another minute.

4. Stir in the rice, mint, salt, saffron strands, cinnamon stick, bay leaves and 1¼ cups of water.

5. Press Cancel to turn off Sauté mode, close the lid and set the Instant Pot® on Rice mode (12 minutes).

6. When cooking time is complete, allow for Natural Pressure Release for 10 minutes or longer, then use Quick Release for any residual pressure. Open and savor this bright, fragrant rice with a salad or Raita (page 239).

Thakkali Shadum Bhaat
Rice with Tomatoes, Curry Leaves, and Peanuts

This style of stir-frying rice with a few characteristic ingredients such as asafoetida, mustard seeds, and curry leaves is common in Tamil Nadu in South India. This rice dish features various vegetables, is often served alongside plain white rice and vegetables, and can be made with leftover rice, much like Chinese-style fried rice. It's easy to make in the Instant Pot® though, and its flavor is much deeper too.

SERVES	TOTAL TIME: 40 MINUTES	DIETARY
4 to 6	Prep Time: 5 minutes Sauté Time: 5 minutes Rice Mode: 12 minutes Pressure Release: about 15 minutes	

INGREDIENTS

2 tablespoons coconut oil

1 teaspoon mustard seeds

1 teaspoon white split lentils (white urad dal)

1 teaspoon split Bengal gram lentils (chana dal)

¼ teaspoon asafoetida

1 tablespoon freshly grated ginger

2 or 3 whole dried red chilies

8 to 10 fresh curry leaves

1 teaspoon ground turmeric

4 tomatoes, diced

1 cup white basmati rice

1 teaspoon salt, or to taste

¼ cup skinless peanuts

2 tablespoons fresh lime juice

1 tablespoon chopped cilantro

INSTRUCTIONS

1. Set the Instant Pot® on medium Sauté mode and heat the oil until the display registers hot, then add the mustard seeds and lentils. Wait until the mustard seeds begin to crackle, then add the asafoetida, ginger, dried red chilies, curry leaves, and turmeric. Sauté well for about 30 seconds.

2. Stir in the tomatoes, rice, salt, and ½ cup of water.

3. Press Cancel to turn off Sauté mode, close the lid, and set the Instant Pot® on Rice mode (12 minutes). When cooking time is complete, allow for Natural Pressure Release for about 15 minutes.

4. In the meantime, toast the peanuts in a skillet until pale golden.

5. Once the pressure is released, remove the lid and stir in the toasted peanuts and lime juice. Remove to a serving bowl, garnish with the cilantro, and serve hot.

Chingri Biryani
Shrimp and Brown Rice Casserole

This is a lovely biryani from North India that I have adapted to a fuss-free wholesome variation done in the Instant Pot®. I am always impressed with how well brown rice works in the Instant Pot®. This biryani cooks up to a nice, light consistency and is perfect with raita or a salad. Leftovers are also great in the lunchbox.

SERVES	TOTAL TIME: 35 MINUTES	DIETARY
4 to 6	Prep Time: 5 minutes Sauté Time: 7 minutes Pressure Cook: 8 minutes Pressure Release: 10 to 15 minutes	

INGREDIENTS

3 tablespoons canola or grapeseed oil

1 large red onion, thinly sliced

1 tablespoon minced fresh ginger

½ tablespoon minced garlic

1 tablespoon garam masala (page 31 or storebought)

½ teaspoon cayenne pepper powder

2 bay leaves

3 or 4 whole cloves

1 large (about 3 inches) cinnamon stick

1½ pounds large shrimp, shelled and deveined

¼ cup tomato sauce

1 cup brown basmati rice

1 teaspoon salt

½ cup raisins

¼ cup chopped nuts

1 tablespoon ghee (optional)

To garnish:

Additional chopped nuts

Chopped cilantro

INSTRUCTIONS

1. Set the Instant Pot® on Sauté mode and heat the oil. When it is hot, add the onions and cook until they are soft and pale golden.

2. Add the ginger and garlic and sauté for about 1 minute. Add the garam masala, cayenne pepper powder, bay leaves, cloves, cinnamon stick, and shrimp and mix well.

3. Stir in the tomato sauce, rice, and 1½ cups of water. Stir in the salt, raisins, and chopped nuts.

4. Press Cancel to turn off the Sauté mode, close the lid, and set the Instant Pot® on Manual Pressure for 8 minutes.

5. When cooking time is complete, allow for Natural Pressure Release for 10 minutes before using Quick Release for any residual pressure.

6. Once pressure is released, remove the lid, stir well, and stir in the ghee, if using. Put rice in a serving bowl, garnish with the nuts and cilantro, and serve hot.

Khichuri
Bengali Red Lentil Risotto

———

A khichuri (or khichdi) is a classic rice and lentil mélange, prepared differently all over India. This particular red lentil variation is from Bengal. It is distinct in its use of fried onions to imbue rich flavor and cauliflower, potatoes, green peas, and a beautiful drizzle of cumin-scented ghee round out this hearty, comforting dish. To make this dish vegan, you can use coconut oil instead of the ghee.

SERVES	TOTAL TIME: 35 MINUTES	DIETARY
4 to 6	Prep Time: 5 minutes Sauté Time: 7 minutes / 1 minute Pressure Cook (Low): 4 minutes Pressure Release: 15 minutes Tempering Time: 1 minute	

INGREDIENTS

4 tablespoons vegetable oil

1 medium red onion, thinly sliced

¾ cup red split lentils (masoor dal)

½ cup basmati or kalajeera rice

1 teaspoon ground cumin

1 teaspoon ground coriander

1 tablespoon grated fresh ginger

½ teaspoon cayenne pepper powder

1 teaspoon salt, or to taste

½ teaspoon ground turmeric

2 cups cauliflower florets

1 medium Yukon gold potato, peeled and cubed

½ cup frozen green peas

For tempering:

1 tablespoon ghee or coconut oil

1½ teaspoons cumin seeds

½ teaspoon dried crushed red pepper (optional)

2 whole dried red chilies

2 tablespoons fresh lime juice

1 tablespoon chopped cilantro

INSTRUCTIONS

1. Set the Instant Pot® on Sauté mode and heat the oil for about 1 minute, then add the onion and sauté until they turn golden, about 5 to 6 minutes. Stir in the lentils, rice, cumin, coriander, ginger, cayenne pepper powder, salt, and turmeric. Add the cauliflower, potato, and 4 cups of water and stir well.

2. Press Cancel to turn off Sauté mode, close the lid, and set the Instant Pot® on Manual Low Pressure mode for 4 minutes.

3. When cooking time is complete, allow for Natural Pressure Release for 10 to 15 minutes, then use Quick Release for any residual pressure.

4. Once pressure is released, open pot and stir rice mixture well. Set the Instant Pot® to Sauté mode and stir in the green peas and cook for 1 minute.

5. To finish, heat the ghee or coconut oil in a small pan, add the cumin seeds, crushed red pepper, if using, and whole dried red chilies and cook until the mixture crackles and is fragrant, being careful not to burn the crushed red pepper. Pour the fragrant mixture over the khichuri and gently stir. Sprinkle on the lime juice and garnish with cilantro before serving.

Awadhi Gosht Biryani
Layered Lamb and Rice Casserole

Biryanis were brought to India by Moghul rulers, who despite arriving from the Middle East, held Central Asia as their ancestral homeland. Biryani varieties that are similar to those in Central Asia are found in Lucknow and Old Delhi as these parts of the country were the heartland of the Moghul kingdom. Over time, the concept of cooking rice and meat and even vegetables together was adopted by other parts of the country. This is one of the more complex recipes in this book. If you follow my suggested sequence, however, you will be done with very little hands-on time.

SERVES	TOTAL TIME: 90 MINUTES	DIETARY
4 to 6	Prep Time: 15 minutes Sauté Time: 20 minutes Rice Mode (twice): 24 minutes Pressure Release (twice): 30 minutes	

INGREDIENTS

For lamb:

1 cup plain yogurt

1-inch piece of ginger, peeled

2 or 3 cloves garlic

1 teaspoon cayenne pepper powder

1½ teaspoons salt

1½ pounds lamb, cubed and trimmed of all visible fat

INSTRUCTIONS

Prepare the lamb:

1. Place the yogurt, ginger, garlic, cayenne pepper powder, and salt in a blender and blend until smooth. In a large zip-top bag or bowl, combine the marinade with the lamb and set aside to marinate while the rice is cooking.

> *Note:*
>
> If you have time to prepare ahead of time , feel free to marinate the lamb in the refrigerator overnight, as this will result in more fragrant and flavorful meat.

For saffron rice:

¾ cup basmati rice

1 teaspoon saffron strands

1 teaspoon ghee (page 27)

1 teaspoon salt

For Essential Rice Layer:

3 tablespoons oil

2 large red onions, thinly sliced

2 or 3 bay leaves

3 green cardamom pods

2 black cardamom pods

1 tablespoon Biryani Masala
  (page 33 or storebought)

1 teaspoon cayenne pepper
  powder (optional)

1½ teaspoons salt, or to taste

2 tomatoes, diced

1 cup basmati rice

For garnish:

½ cup raisins

¼ cup slivered pistachios

⅓ cup sliced almonds

Prepare the saffron rice:

2. Place all the ingredients for the saffron rice plus ⅔ cup of water in the Instant Pot®. Close the lid, and set on Rice mode (12 minutes). When cooking time is complete, allow for Natural Pressure Release for about 10 to 15 minutes. Remove the saffron rice from the Instant Pot® and set aside. Rinse and dry the insert bowl.

Prepare Essential Rice Layer:

3. Place the insert back into the Instant Pot® and set on Sauté mode. Pour in the oil and after it heats for about 1 minute, add the onions. Cook the onions for about 10 minutes, until they wilt and turn golden brown.

4. Remove half the onions and set aside for later use. To the remaining onions add the bay leaves, cardamom pods, and marinated lamb pieces, reserving the marinade.

5. Stir in the biryani masala, cayenne pepper powder (if using), and salt, and cook for about 3 minutes. Add the tomatoes and reserved lamb marinade and cook for another 2 minutes. Add the rice and ½ cup of water and mix well.

6. Press Cancel to turn off the Sauté mode. Close the lid and set the Instant Pot® to the Rice mode (12 minutes). When cooking time is complete, allow for Natural Pressure Release for about 15 minutes.

Finish dish:

7. Once the pressure is released, remove the cover and gently stir in the saffron rice.

8. Put rice in a serving bowl and garnish with the raisins, pistachios, and almonds. Serve with a side of Raita (page 239).

Misthi Pulao
Bengali Festive Golden Pilaf

This delicate, slightly sweet rice is a festive Bengali pilaf, usually served as an accompaniment to more complex, rich meat dishes. It is traditionally made with kalajeera rice and a lot of ghee but I make this with everyday basmati rice as a treat sometimes. The Instant Pot® cuts out any fuss and delivers a perfectly cooked, impressive rice in less than twenty minutes. To make this recipe vegan, you can simply substitute coconut oil for the ghee.

SERVES	TOTAL TIME: 35 MINUTES	DIETARY
4 to 6	Prep Time: 5 minutes Sauté Time: 3 minutes Rice Mode: 12 minutes Pressure Release: 15 minutes	

INGREDIENTS

1 tablespoon ghee (page 27) or coconut oil

2 large bay leaves

4 or 5 whole cloves

3 or 4 green cardamom pods

2 star anise (optional)

1 large (about 4-inch) cinnamon stick

1½ cups basmati rice

¾ teaspoon ground turmeric

1 teaspoon salt

1½ teaspoons sugar

2 tablespoons slivered almonds

1 tablespoon raw unsalted cashews

1½ tablespoons assorted raisins

INSTRUCTIONS

1. Set the Instant Pot® on Sauté mode and heat the ghee or coconut oil for about 1 minute. Add the bay leaves, cloves, cardamom pods, star anise, if using, and cinnamon stick, and stir for 1 minute until the spices darken a little.

2. Add the basmati rice, turmeric, salt, sugar, almonds, cashews, and raisins and mix well. Stir in about 1½ cups of water.

3. Press Cancel to turn off the Sauté mode and close the lid. Set the Instant Pot® to Rice mode (12 minutes).

4. When cooking time is complete, allow for Natural Pressure Release after about 10 minutes, then use Quick Release for any residual pressure. Open the lid, and serve immediately.

Chettinad Kozhi Biryani
Chicken Coconut Rice with Fennel

——

The Chettinad community of Tamil Nadu in Southern India showcases exceptional meat-and-fish-based cuisine. This nicely compliments the unique vegetarian dishes that are found throughout the rest of the state. This biryani is traditionally made with a rice variety called Seeraga Samba, but basmati rice works as a good substitute. I personally love the nuanced delicate spicing of this recipe, which is simpler than North Indian biryani variations. Traditionally, this is garnished with whole or halved hard-boiled eggs. Chicken on the bone is usually best for this recipe, but boneless skinless chicken thighs will work in a pinch.

SERVES	TOTAL TIME: 45 MINUTES	DIETARY
4 to 6	Prep Time: 8 minutes Sauté Time: 10 minutes Rice Mode: 12 minutes Pressure Release: 15 minutes	

INGREDIENTS

For chicken marinade:

1½ teaspoons fennel seeds

1 large (2 inch) cinnamon stick

6 to 8 whole cloves

4 to 6 green cardamom pods

1 tablespoon grated fresh ginger

1 tablespoon grated garlic

¾ cup thick plain yogurt

1 teaspoon salt

¼ teaspoon ground turmeric

1 teaspoon cayenne pepper powder

1½ pounds skinless chicken pieces, on the bone

INSTRUCTIONS

Marinate chicken:

1. Grind the fennel seeds, cinnamon stick, cloves, and cardamom pods into a fine powder in a spice mill or coffee grinder. Place in a large bowl and mix in the ginger, garlic, yogurt, salt, turmeric, and cayenne pepper powder. Cut the chicken pieces in half and add to the marinade and toss to coat. Set aside to marinate while you continue with the rest of the preparation.

For rice:

2 tablespoon canola oil or ghee (page 27)

1 or 2 bay leaves

3 or 4 whole cloves

2 star anise

1 cinnamon stick (about 2 inches)

1 large onion, thinly sliced

2 medium tomatoes, pureed

$\frac{1}{3}$ cup whole fresh mint leaves

$\frac{1}{3}$ cup finely chopped cilantro

$\frac{3}{4}$ cup coconut milk

1½ cups white basmati rice

1 teaspoon salt

Make biryani:

2. Set the Instant Pot® to Sauté mode, and heat the oil or ghee for 1 minute. The pot should say hot. Add the bay leaves, cloves, star anise, and cinnamon stick and let them sizzle a little. Add the sliced onion and sauté for 6 to 7 minutes, until the onion is wilted and turning brown.

3. Add the marinated chicken and mix well. Stir in the pureed tomatoes, mint, cilantro, and coconut milk. Stir in the rice and salt.

4. Press Cancel to turn off the Sauté mode. Close the lid, and set Instant Pot® to Rice mode (12 minutes).

5. When cooking time is complete, allow for Natural Pressure Release for 10 to 15 minutes. Enjoy with Raita (page 239).

Paneer aur Subji Pulao
White Cheese and Mixed Vegetable Pilaf

Though beautiful pulao hails from North India, honestly, it could be from anywhere in India. Every home has a version, where a chockful of vegetables are thrown in with some fragrant spices to make a one-pot meal, maybe with a side of yogurt and lentils, which are omnipresent on the Indian table. In my home, I like to add fresh homemade paneer since my daughter, while eschewing meat, loves dairy and fish. On busy days if you have a packet of frozen organic mixed vegetables around, you can make this dish without any major chopping.

SERVES

4 to 6

TOTAL TIME: 45 MINUTES
Prep Time: 3 minutes
Sauté Time: 10 minutes
Rice Mode: 12 minutes
Pressure Release: 15 minutes

DIETARY

INGREDIENTS

2 tablespoons oil or ghee (page 27)

1 teaspoon cumin seeds

3 or 4 whole cloves

2 or 3 bay leaves

2 black cardamom pods

1 large cinnamon stick, broken into small pieces

1 onion, thinly sliced

1½ cups white basmati rice

1½ teaspoons salt

½ teaspoon saffron strands (optional)

1 teaspoon sugar

1½ cups assorted vegetables, chopped or sliced if needed (carrots, peas, green beans are all good ideas)

1 cup cubed fresh paneer (page 26)

1 or 2 tablespoons sliced almonds

INSTRUCTIONS

1. Set the Instant Pot® on Sauté mode on high. Heat the oil or ghee for 1 minute until the pot registers hot. Add the cumin seeds, cloves, bay leaves, cardamom pods, and cinnamon stick, and stir lightly.

2. Add the onion and sauté for about 5 to 7 minutes. Add the rice, salt, saffron strands, if using, sugar, vegetables, and paneer. Stir in ¾ cup of water.

3. Press Cancel to turn off the Sauté mode, close the lid, and set Instant Pot® on the Rice mode (12 minutes).

4. When cooking time is complete, allow for Natural Pressure Release for at least 15 minutes. Remove the lid, place rice in a serving bowl, garnish with the sliced almonds, and serve.

Hakka Noodles
Indo-Chinese Mixed Noodles

Noodles tossed with vegetables, chopped eggs, and a spicy assortment of seasonings is the way Indians enjoy their version of Chinese food in their homes and as a popular street food. My mother would make this for us as a relaxed meal, especially when my father was traveling. I make this popular and fun dish often, and thanks to the Instant Pot®, I am able to tackle it in less than twenty minutes. Noodles from an Indian grocery work well for this dish (my preferred brand is Ching's), but it can be made with any unseasoned quick-cooking noodles of your choice. In fact, in a pinch I have made this with angel hair pasta. You can also use gluten-free noodles, if desired.

SERVES	TOTAL TIME: 20 MINUTES	DIETARY
4 to 6	Prep Time: 7 minutes Sauté Time: 3 minutes Pressure Cook: 1 minute Cook Time: 2 minutes	

INGREDIENTS

1 tablespoon soy sauce

1 tablespoon white vinegar

1 tablespoon chili garlic sauce (such as Sriracha)

1 teaspoon sugar

3 tablespoons oil

3 cloves garlic, minced

1 tablespoon grated fresh ginger

1 onion, thinly sliced

12 ounces dried thin noodles

2 eggs

1 teaspoon salt

1 bell pepper, minced

2 carrots, peeled and grated

1 tablespoon chopped cilantro

4 green onions or scallions, chopped

INSTRUCTIONS

1. Mix the soy sauce, vinegar, chili garlic sauce, and sugar in a small bowl and set aside.

2. Set the Instant Pot® on Sauté mode. Heat about 1½ tablespoons of the oil in the pot for 1 minute. Add the garlic, ginger, and onion and sauté for 2 minutes. Press Cancel to turn off Sauté mode.

3. Stir in the noodles, reserved soy sauce mixture, and about ¾ cup of water. Set the Instant Pot® on Manual Pressure mode for 1 minute.

4. In the meantime, in a frying pan heat the remaining 1½ tablespoons of oil. Beat the eggs with the salt and pour into the pan. Spread flat and cook until set. Remove and cut into small pieces.

5. When pressure cooking time is complete, do a Quick Pressure Release. Once the pressure is released, open the lid, add the bell pepper, carrots, and chopped egg and mix well. Put the noodle mixture in a serving dish, garnish with the cilantro and green onions, and serve immediately.

LEGUMES
& SOUPS

Legumes/dals/lentils/pulses round out offerings on the Indian table.
There are countless varieties of legumes that provide much-needed,
comforting protein in a largely vegetarian diet. These legumes are usually
grouped in the general category of dal. While there is no one variety of
dal, it is a broad enough food group to have some very basic and general
rules, which I cover in my Indian Legumes Primer (page 89). Other than
providing a good source of protein and essential amino acids, legumes
offer a wealth of dietary fiber, vitamins, and minerals, and are an excellent
source of iron.

India is responsible for almost half of the world's legume production.
Legumes are one of the oldest cultivated crops in the world, going back

to well over three thousand years. In India, they are mainly used in their dried, split, and husked form (*dal*), but sometimes are used un-husked (*sabut*). The unhusked varieties tend to find favor among North Indians.

Dishes made with split lentils usually go under the generic name "*dal*," with the variety of the lentil distinguishing the dish, such as *Masoor Dal* or *Moong Dal*. With more complex varieties, such as whole beans, red kidney beans, and chickpeas, the dishes are usually given a distinct name such as *Choley* (chickpeas) or *Rajmah* (red kidney beans). Most of these legumes lose their vivid coloring when cooked, but they do have very distinct tastes.

Legumes are an element that weaves all the diverse culinary influences in Indian cuisine together. While cooked differently in various parts of India, a good Indian meal anywhere is incomplete without some dal.

Indians have an interesting relationship with soups. Though soups do not officially feature as a part of the meal sequence, they exist on the Indian table as a vestige of the colonial influence. They are popular as a course in a formal meal or certainly in winter. I have included a couple in this chapter to give you an idea of some Indian soups.

Indian Legumes Primer

TO SOAK OR NOT TO SOAK

Conventional time-tested wisdom in the Indian kitchen suggests that you soak the skinned legumes and beans for a few hours before cooking. More does not hurt. For a quick soak you can pour boiling water over them and soak for about an hour. Soaking helps with removing some insoluble toxins and also allows the beans to cook into a soft, plump consistency.

FREEZING COOKED BEANS FOR A RAINY DAY

Drained cooked beans such as chickpeas, red kidney beans, and black beans can be frozen and used just like canned beans when needed. This offers the convenience without the added sodium or preservatives found with canned beans.

TEMPERING AND SEASONING BEANS AND LENTILS

While there are many ways to cook and season beans and lentils, the most common is to heat oil, bloom a few whole spices and aromatics, and pour this mixture over the cooked legumes. Another good option is to simmer with my Everyday Masala Paste (page 29).

Glossary of Indian Legumes

Adzuki Beans / Chotey Rajma: Quick cooking, highly nutritious adzuki beans make a good quick-cook substitute for traditional kidney beans and can be used in any recipe of your choice.

Black-Eyed Peas / Lobia: The black-eyed pea plant was first domesticated in West Africa. The legume pods are light beige in color with black middles or "eyes." These are popular in several cultures as well as in India. In the southern United States, black-eyed peas are considered a lucky way to start the New Year. Recommended tempering: onion masala.
Instant Pot®: Bean/Chili setting 15 minutes (pre-soaking is highly recommended)

Black Lentils / Sabut Urad Dal: Small whole dried black lentils are the Indian version of black beans. They can be cooked the same way as in any black bean recipes. Slow simmered for hours in North Indian kitchens, these lentils have a satisfying texture that works well in soups or stews.

Brown Lentils / Sabut Masoor Dal: I like to call these "lentil soup lentils" since they are most commonly used for lentil soups in American, Mediterranean, and various other cuisines. In Northern India, you'll find these dried whole brown lentils used in comforting lentil stews and served with rice or handmade flatbreads. Recommended tempering: chopped garlic, whole cumin seeds.
Instant Pot®: Bean/Chili setting 12 minutes (pre-soaking is highly recommended)

Cannellini Beans / Safed Rajma: My family is very fond of these beans, so I include them in our culinary repertoire. Their softer and milder texture makes them a good addition for delicate cooking.

Chana Dal / Split Bengal Gram Lentils / Dried Split Chickpeas: This yellow lentil looks a lot like yellow split peas, but has a nuttier and more complex taste. Its thicker consistency makes it a good option for fritters, veggie burgers, and other hearty offerings.

Chickpeas / Garbanzo Beans / Kabuli Chola: These beige legumes are popular in North Indian and Middle Eastern cuisine. They are low maintenance since they grow with very little water and are therefore a boon to drier, desert-like climates. Less common brown chickpeas have an interesting taste and can be used the same way as yellow chickpeas. Recommended tempering: onion masala.
Instant Pot®: Bean/Chili setting 45 minutes (pre-soaking is highly recommended)

Green Lentils / Sabut Moong Dal: Whole green lentils are usually cooked in dry preparations. They are my favorite lentil for sprouting and using in salads. They also work well in recipes for lentil pancakes and rice and lentil pilafs.

Orange/Red Split Lentils / Masoor Dal: Orange/red split lentils are one of the most common lentils in my kitchen, due to their quick cooking time. They cook up to buttery softness and can be finished nicely with some light tempering or even just a touch of butter or ghee. Recommended tempering: chopped fried onions.
Instant Pot®: Pressure setting 5 minutes

Red Kidney Beans / Rajma: Named because of their indented shape resembling a human kidney, these beans have a dark red color making them rich in both antioxidants and iron. They cook up to a nice comforting softness. Recommended tempering: whole cumin seeds, lime juice.
Instant Pot®: Bean/Chili setting 30 minutes (pre-soaking is highly recommended)

White Split Lentils / Dhuli Urad Dal: White split lentils are the husked counterpart of whole black lentils and are typically used to make batters for crepes and fritters since they grind up to a soft consistency. They can, of course, be cooked as a lentil stew as well.

Yellow Split Lentils / Dhuli Moong Dal: These split lentils are the husked variety of green lentils. They cook up fairly quickly and tend to have a slightly stronger taste than orange/red lentils. I like to combine these lentils with vegetables. Recommended tempering: whole cumin seeds, lime juice.
Instant Pot®: Pressure setting 5 minutes

Yellow Split Pigeon Peas / Arhar Dal / Toor Dal: These lentils are similar to yellow Bengali gram lentils but have a slightly darker ochre-like color. These lentils have a very distinct, earthy taste. They work well with tart flavors and are usually cooked with a souring agent such as tamarind, lime, or green mango.

Rajma with Adzuki Beans
North Indian Red Bean Curry

———

Rajma is a curried North Indian red kidney bean stew. Served with steamed white rice, it is comfort food reserved for Sunday afternoons. In my household, since people are not all that excited about red kidney beans, I adapted the recipe using smaller, thin-skinned adzuki beans. This is every bit as comforting and delicious, plus adzuki beans are naturally creamy and cook much faster than red kidney beans—a win-win!

SERVES	TOTAL TIME: 25 MINUTES	DIETARY
4 to 6	Prep Time: 5 minutes Sauté Time: 7 minutes Pressure Cook: 10 minutes	

INGREDIENTS

2 tablespoons oil

1 teaspoon cumin seeds

1 red onion, chopped

3 cloves garlic, minced

1 tablespoon grated fresh ginger

1 teaspoon cayenne pepper powder

1 teaspoon ground cumin

1 teaspoon ground coriander

1 cup chopped tomatoes

¾ cup dried red adzuki beans

1½ teaspoons salt, or to taste

1 teaspoon garam masala (page 31 or storebought)

2 tablespoons fresh lime juice

1 tablespoon chopped cilantro

INSTRUCTIONS

1. Set the Instant Pot® to Sauté mode and heat the oil for about 1 minute. Add the cumin seeds and wait until the seeds begin to sizzle. Add the red onion, garlic, and ginger, and sauté until onions are soft and wilted, about 4 minutes.

2. Add the cayenne pepper powder, cumin, and coriander and stir well. Stir in the chopped tomatoes, adzuki beans, salt, and 2 cups of water.

3. Press Cancel to turn off the Sauté mode and close the lid. Set the Instant Pot® to Manual Pressure mode for 15 minutes.

4. When the cooking time is complete, allow for Natural Pressure Release or do a Quick Release if you are in a hurry.

5. Once the pressure is released, remove the cover and stir in the garam masala and lime juice. Place in a serving bowl, garnish with cilantro and serve with steamed rice.

Tarka Dal
Yellow Split Lentils with Tomatoes

Tarka Dal, if you understand the meaning, might sound like an oxymoron. Tarka, or the process of tempering with spices at the end of cooking, is what makes Indian lentils the magical soft pools of goodness that we all love. The process of making dal is incomplete without the tarka, so listing it in the name almost sounds redundant. But the Tarka Dal for the Punjabi table actually reverses this process, instead of finishing with the tarka we start with it, making this dish perfect for fix-and-forget cooking. On a busy evening, you can whip up this amazing pot of goodness, serve it with homemade or store-bought parathas, and you are in business.

SERVES

4 to 6

TOTAL TIME: 20 MINUTES
Prep Time: 6 minutes
Sauté Time: 4 minutes
Pressure Cook: 5 minutes
Pressure Release: 5 minutes

DIETARY

INGREDIENTS

2 tablespoons oil

1 teaspoon cumin seeds

1 teaspoon mustard seeds

1 tablespoon minced fresh ginger

1 tablespoon minced garlic

¾ cup yellow split lentils (moong dal)

3 medium tomatoes, coarsely chopped

½ teaspoon ground turmeric

1 teaspoon cumin coriander powder

1 teaspoon cayenne pepper powder

1 teaspoon salt, or to taste

2 tablespoons fresh lime juice

2 tablespoons chopped cilantro

Crushed red pepper flakes to garnish

INSTRUCTIONS

1. Set the Instant Pot® on Sauté mode and heat the oil for 1 minute. Add the cumin seeds, mustard seeds, ginger, and garlic and sauté until fragrant. Add the lentils and sauté lightly.

2. Stir in 3 cups of water, the tomatoes, turmeric, cumin coriander powder, cayenne pepper powder, and salt.

3. Press Cancel to turn off the Sauté mode. Close the lid and set the Instant Pot® on Manual Pressure for 5 minutes. When the cooking time is complete, allow for Natural Pressure Release for about 5 minutes.

4. Once the pressure is released, open the pot and stir in the lime juice. Garnish with cilantro and crushed red pepper flakes to serve.

Masoor Dal
Red Lentils with Tomatoes and Cilantro

———

On a chilly New York winter evening, I often crave these extremely simple, smooth, buttery lentils. Indeed, Masoor Dal, as this dish is known on the Bengali table (not to be confused with just the lentil itself), is the ultimate comfort food. While the sautéed onions do need to be done separately and take a little bit of time to assemble, I believe this is well worth the effort.

SERVES

4 to 6

TOTAL TIME: 15 MINUTES
Prep Time: 5 minutes
Pressure Cook (Low): 4 minutes
Pressure Release: 5 minutes
Tempering Time: 1 minutes

DIETARY

INGREDIENTS

¾ cup red split lentils (masoor dal)

½ teaspoon ground turmeric

1 teaspoon ground cumin

1 teaspoon salt

1 teaspoon cayenne pepper powder

¾ cup chopped tomatoes

3 tablespoons grapeseed oil

1 medium red onion, chopped

1 teaspoon ghee or coconut oil

1 teaspoon panch phoron (Bengali Five Spice mix)

1 or 2 whole dried red chilies (optional)

2 tablespoons lime or lemon juice

2 tablespoons chopped cilantro

INSTRUCTIONS

1. Place the lentils, turmeric, cumin, salt, cayenne pepper powder, tomatoes, and 2 to 3 cups of water (depending on your preferred thickness) in the Instant Pot®. Close the lid, and set on Manual Low Pressure for 4 minutes.

2. While the lentils are cooking, heat the grapeseed oil in a small skillet and add the onion. Gently sauté for about 6 to 7 minutes until the onion turns pale golden and lightly crisp.

3. When the lentil cooking time is complete, allow for Natural Pressure Release for about 5 minutes. Remove the lid and stir in the cooked onion.

4. Heat the ghee or coconut oil in the skillet and add the panch phoron and red chilies (if using) and cook until they crackle. Pour the ghee mixture over the cooked lentils and gently stir in.

5. Stir in the lemon juice and chopped cilantro and serve hot with steamed rice.

Kala Dal Makhani
Soft Simmered Black Beans

There is an entire series of dishes that fall in the "makhani" category of cooking. The term basically translates to "buttery." These elaborate party dishes are at the core of festive Punjabi cooking and are among the signature dishes of many Indian restaurants. My easy Basic Makhani Masala and Everyday Masala Paste along with regular black beans make this a very accessible indulgence.

SERVES

4 to 6

TOTAL TIME: 4 HOURS & 40 MINUTES
Prep Time: 3 minutes plus 4 hours soaking time
Bean/Chili Mode: 15 minutes
Pressure Release: 15 minutes
Sauté Time: 5 minutes

DIETARY

INGREDIENTS

1 cup dried black beans, soaked for 4 to 6 hours, drained

½ cup Everyday Masala Paste (page 29)

½ cup Basic Makhani Masala (page 30)

1 tablespoon dried fenugreek leaves (kasuri methi)

1 teaspoon garam masala (page 31 or storebought)

⅓ cup fresh cream

2 to 3 tablespoons fresh lime juice

Thinly sliced onions for garnish

INSTRUCTIONS

1. Place the drained black beans, Everyday Masala Paste, Basic Makhani Masala, and 1 cup of water in the Instant Pot®. Close the lid, set on Bean/Chili mode for 15 minutes. When cooking time is complete, allow for Natural Pressure Release for 15 minutes. Remove the lid and stir well.

2. Set the Instant Pot® on the Sauté mode and bring to a simmer. The beans should be soft and the mixture should be saucy rather than thin. If the sauce appears thin, cook for a few minutes to thicken it.

3. Stir in the dried fenugreek leaves and garam masala and simmer for 5 minutes. Mix in the cream, reserving a little to drizzle over the top.

4. Place the beans in a serving bowl. Sprinkle with the lime juice, thinly sliced onions, and remaining cream. Serve with rice or your favorite flatbread.

Sambhar

South Indian Pigeon Pea Stew with Vegetables

———

Sambhar is a classic South Indian stew, made several times a week if not every day in most South Indian households. A sambhar can be made in a multitude of ways, with every imaginable assortment of vegetable-and-bean combinations. At the heart of the dish, however, is a good sambhar masala—a versatile and somewhat complex seasoning blend. I provide my recipe for this spice blend, but you can also use a storebought variety. Tamarind paste is another integral ingredient, to give the sambhar its characteristic tartness. It is important for the lentils to be soupy and smooth, and that the vegetables not get overcooked, so resist the urge to add everything at the same time.

SERVES	TOTAL TIME: 25 MINUTES	DIETARY
4 to 6	Prep Time: 10 minutes Pressure Cook: 8 minutes Sauté Time: 5 minutes Tempering Time: 2 minutes	

INGREDIENTS

½ cup yellow split pigeon peas (toor dal)

1 tablespoon Sambhar Masala (page 32 or store bought)

2 teaspoons salt

½ cup tomato sauce or fresh tomato puree

1½ cups chopped assorted vegetables (such as beans, carrots, peas, etc.)

1½ tablespoons tamarind paste

For tempering:

2 tablespoons oil

¼ teaspoon asafoetida

¾ teaspoon mustard seeds

12 curry leaves

2 or 3 whole dried red chilies

3 tablespoons chopped cilantro

INSTRUCTIONS

1. Place the pigeon peas, sambhar masala, 1 teaspoon of the salt, tomato sauce, and 2½ cups of water in the Instant Pot®. Close the lid and set on Manual Pressure mode for 8 minutes. When the cooking time is complete, do a Quick Pressure Release.

2. Remove the lid and stir well. The sambhar should not be too thick or too thin (about the consistency of a cream soup). Add the remaining 1 teaspoon of salt and the vegetables. Mix the tamarind paste with about ½ cup of water and stir into the sambhar.

3. Set the Instant Pot® on the Sauté mode and allow the sambhar to simmer until the vegetables are tender, about 5 minutes. Taste for seasonings.

4. Heat the oil in a small skillet and add the asafoetida and mustard seeds. When the mustard seeds begin to crackle, add the curry leaves and dried red chilies. After a few seconds pour the seasoned oil over the prepared sambhar and stir well.

5. Stir in the cilantro and enjoy with rice or any of the breakfast dishes such as Idlis (page 43) or Masala Dosas (page 47).

Langar Ki Dal
Community Kitchen Traditional Lentils

The Sikh community, originating in Punjab, incorporates community service as one of their key principles of living. This is manifested in the fact that Gurudwaras (Sikh temples) offer free community meals called langars. *The hallmark of the langar meal is typically this simple wholesome stew of mixed lentils gently seasoned with ghee and ginger. The lentils cook for a long time to achieve the dishes rich consistency. We are able to do this without much fuss in the Instant Pot®. This meal is completed with hearty whole wheat flatbreads, raw red onions, and yogurt. I first encountered this dish when visiting the city of Amritsar in Punjab, and cook this anytime I want to bring the warmth and simplicity of that city into my home.*

SERVES	TOTAL TIME: 45 MINUTES (plus 6 hours for soaking lentils)	DIETARY
4 to 6	Prep Time: 5 minutes Sauté Time: 5 minutes Bean/Chili Mode: 25 minutes Pressure Release: 10 minutes	

INGREDIENTS

2 tablespoons ghee (page 27)

1 teaspoon cumin seeds

1 tablespoon grated fresh ginger

2 green chilies, minced

2 tomatoes, chopped

1½ teaspoons ground coriander

¾ cup black lentils (black whole urad dal), soaked for 6 hours

⅓ cup split Bengal gram lentils (chana dal), soaked for 6 hours

1½ to 2 teaspoons salt

2 tablespoons chopped cilantro

INSTRUCTIONS

1. Set the Instant Pot® on Sauté mode and heat the ghee until the Instant Pot® registers hot. Add the cumin seeds and wait until the seeds sizzle. Add the ginger, green chilies, and tomatoes and cook until they are somewhat soft. Stir in the coriander, both lentils, salt, and 3 cups water.

2. Press Cancel to turn off the Sauté mode. Close the lid and set the Instant Pot® on Bean/Chili mode for 25 minutes.

3. When cooking time is complete, allow for Natural Pressure Release for about 10 minutes.

4. Once the pressure is released, remove the cover and stir the dal. It should be soft and thick. Stir in the cilantro and serve.

Konkani Lobia
Tangy Black-Eyed Peas

———

Another favorite in the Indian pulse arsenal are black-eyed peas. This variation is from the coastal cuisine of the Konkan region of southwestern India. The tangy black-eyed peas are often accentuated with pieces of squash or elephant yams. It is difficult to find elephant yams in U.S. markets, so I use a medley of zucchini and butternut squash. This simple, delicate recipe with its flavors of sweet and tart is one of our favorite meals.

SERVES	TOTAL TIME: 50 MINUTES	DIETARY
4 to 6	Prep Time: 5 minutes plus 30 minutes soaking time Sauté Time: 5 minutes Pressure Cook (twice): 11 minutes	

INGREDIENTS

1 tablespoon oil

1 teaspoon black mustard seeds

8 to 10 curry leaves

1 teaspoon ground cumin

1 teaspoon ground coriander

3 tomatoes, chopped

1 teaspoon cayenne pepper powder

¾ cup black-eyed peas, soaked for 30 minutes

1 teaspoon salt

1 cup cubed butternut squash

1 cup cubed green zucchini

1 tablespoon tamarind paste

½ cup coconut milk

INSTRUCTIONS

1. Set the Instant Pot® to Sauté mode, and heat the oil until the pot registers hot. Add the mustard seeds, wait until they crackle, and then add the curry leaves, cumin, coriander, and tomatoes, and cook until soft.

2. Stir in the cayenne pepper powder, black-eyed peas, salt, and 1½ cups of water.

3. Press Cancel to turn off Sauté mode. Close the lid and set Instant Pot® on Manual Pressure mode for 9 minutes. When the cooking time is complete, do a Quick Pressure Release.

4. Once the pressure is released, open the lid, and stir in the butternut squash, zucchini, and tamarind paste. Close the lid and set on Manual Pressure mode for 2 minutes. When cooking time is complete, do Quick Pressure Release. Enjoy with rice or flatbreads.

Pindi Dhaba Choley
Dark and Spicy Indian Truckstop Chickpeas

A chapter on Indian pulses would be incomplete without a recipe for chickpeas. This particular recipe does have Punjabi roots, but is named after the Pakistani city of Rawalpindi. It is something that I have successfully mastered and simplified without compromising its authenticity. The list of ingredients might seem daunting, but most of them are just added to the mix. Before you complain, let me tell you the original version had at least four stages of different cooking which I have culled down to a one-pot dish.

SERVES

4 to 6

TOTAL TIME: 70 MINUTES (plus 4 hours for soaking chickpeas)
Prep Time: 5 minutes
Sauté Time: 7 minutes
Bean/Chili Mode: 45 minutes
Pressure Release: 5 minutes
Additional Sauté Time: 5 minutes (optional)

DIETARY

INGREDIENTS

¼ cup oil

2 or 3 dried bay leaves

1 medium red onion, finely chopped

2 tablespoons grated fresh ginger

1 tablespoon minced garlic

¾ cup dried chickpeas, soaked for 4 hours or overnight

1 teaspoon cayenne pepper powder

1 teaspoon freshly ground black pepper

1 tablespoon dried mango powder (amchur powder)

1 tablespoon dried fenugreek leaves (kasuri methi)

1½ tablespoons garam masala

1 teaspoon salt

1 teaspoon ground coriander

½ cup tomato puree (fresh or canned)

Garnishes

2 tablespoons fresh lime juice

Thinly sliced strips of fresh ginger

1 tablespoon chopped cilantro (optional)

INSTRUCTIONS

1. Set the Instant Pot® on Sauté mode and add the oil. After a minute, add the bay leaves and cook for a few seconds. Add the onion, ginger, and garlic and sauté for 4 minutes.

2. Add the chickpeas and stir well. Add the cayenne pepper powder, ground black pepper, mango powder, fenugreek leaves, garam masala, salt, ground coriander, and tomato puree and bring to a simmer.

3. Press Cancel to turn off the Sauté mode and stir in 1 cup of water. Close the lid and set the Instant Pot® on Bean/Chili mode for 45 minutes.

4. When cooking time is complete, allow for Natural Pressure Release for 5 minutes and then use Quick Release for any redisual pressure. Open the lid and stir well. If the mixture is very watery you may want to set it on Sauté mode and cook off the water.

5. Stir in the lime juice and garnish with the ginger and cilantro and serve.

Tamatar Shorba
Indian Tomato Soup

———

Various types of tomato soups are popular on the Indian table. This particular recipe is my mother's and something that I crave anytime I need a little extra comforting. In fact, the last time I visited India, I followed her around to master the steps and ingredients. Since she uses a pressure cooker for this recipe anyway, adapting this for the Instant Pot® was easy.

SERVES	TOTAL TIME: 10 MINUTES	DIETARY
4 to 6	Prep Time: 5 minutes Pressure Cook: 4 minutes	

INGREDIENTS

10 medium tomatoes, quartered

1 large carrot, chopped

1 teaspoon salt

1½ teaspoons sugar

1 teaspoon cayenne pepper powder

1 tablespoon grated fresh ginger

3 cloves garlic, minced

1 teaspoon ground coriander

2 teaspoons ground black pepper

½ cup heavy cream

Chopped cilantro

INSTRUCTIONS

1. Place the tomatoes, carrot, salt, sugar, cayenne pepper powder, ginger, garlic, coriander, and black pepper in the Instant Pot®. Add 1½ cups of water.

2. Close the lid and set the Instant Pot® on Manual Pressure for 4 minutes. When the cooking time is complete, do a Quick Pressure Release.

3. Once the pressure is released, remove the cover. Using an immersion blender, blend the soup until smooth. Stir in the cream. Serve garnished with cilantro.

Pahari Kadhi
Chickpea and Yogurt Soup

A kadhi (not to be confused with kari/curry) is a delicately seasoned yogurt-and-chickpea soup or stew, prepared differently in various parts of India. A highly nutritious, protein-rich creation, this nourishing dish is at the heart of a good vegetarian meal. This version, from the highland state of Himachal, is simple and comforting. I have added in garlic chives for a nice, nuanced hint of flavor.

SERVES	TOTAL TIME: 15 MINUTES	DIETARY
4 to 6	Prep Time: 5 minutes Sauté Time: 4 minutes Pressure Cook (Low): 3 minutes	

INGREDIENTS

⅓ cup chickpea flour (besan)

2 cups plain yogurt

1 tablespoon canola or grapeseed oil

1 teaspoon cumin seeds

1 teaspoon mustard seeds

1 tablespoon grated fresh ginger

2 whole dried red chilies

8 to 10 curry leaves

½ teaspoon ground turmeric

1 teaspoon salt

½ cup chopped fresh garlic chives

1 tablespoon chopped cilantro

INSTRUCTIONS

1. In a mixing bowl, whisk the chickpea flour, breaking up all the lumps (this is important for a good, smooth soup). Add the yogurt and 2 cups of water and mix well.

2. Set the Instant Pot® on Sauté mode and heat the oil. Add the cumin seeds and mustard seeds and wait until the mustard seeds begin to crackle. Add the ginger and stir lightly. Add the red chilies and curry leaves and stir lightly. Stir in the turmeric and salt, and pour in the chickpea flour mixture and stir well.

3. Press Cancel to turn off the Sauté mode, close the lid, and set the Instant Pot® on Manual Low Pressure for 3 minutes.

4. When cooking time is complete, do a Quick Pressure Release. Remove the cover, stir in the garlic chives and cilantro, and serve with hot freshly steamed rice.

Thukpa
Curried Vegetable Noodle Soup

This hearty, full-flavored soup hails from the northeastern highlands of India, as well as from the mountain state of Ladakh, which borders Tibet. You can pretty much add any vegetables that catch your fancy. I use an assortment of what I have readily available, and this soup is usually a hit with my family during chilly late winter or early spring evenings in New York.

SERVES	TOTAL TIME: 15 MINUTES	DIETARY
4 to 6	Prep Time: 5 minutes Sauté Time: 3 minutes / 5 minutes Pressure Cook: 1 minute	

INGREDIENTS

2 tablespoons mustard oil

1 medium onion, chopped

4 green onions, minced, greens and whites kept separate

1 tablespoon minced garlic

2 tomatoes, minced

1 teaspoon ground cumin

1 teaspoon garam masala (page 31 or storebought)

1 teaspoon freshly ground black pepper

2 teaspoons salt, or to taste

4 cups water or vegetable broth

1 cup cauliflower florets

1 medium carrot, peeled and chopped

1 medium potato, peeled and chopped

2 to 4 radishes, thinly sliced

10 to 12 ounces angel hair pasta or rice noodles

1 cup baby spinach

½ cup cilantro, minced

4 tablespoons freshly squeezed lemon juice

INSTRUCTIONS

1. Set the Instant Pot® to Sauté mode and heat the mustard oil. Add the onion, scallion whites, and garlic and sauté lightly. Stir in the tomatoes, cumin, garam masala, black pepper, salt, and 4 cups of water or broth. Add the cauliflower, carrot, potato, and radishes.

2. Press Cancel to turn off Sauté mode. Close the lid and set the Instant Pot® on Manual Pressure for 1 minute. When cooking time is complete, use Quick Pressure Release. Once the pressure is released, open the lid.

3. Set the Instant Pot® on Sauté mode and stir in the pasta. When pasta is cooked, press Cancel to turn off the Sauté mode.

4. Stir in the spinach, cilantro, and reserved green onions. Sprinkle with lemon juice and serve as a wholesome one-pot meal.

Carrot and Beetroot Rasam
Spicy Carrot Beet Soup

———

A rasam is a thin, broth-like soup from southern India. It is made with vegetables like tomatoes and beets. In this recipe, I have drawn inspiration by using traditional rasam spices, but have kept this full-bodied by adding almonds for a creamy, nutritious punch. This vivid pink soup will bring brightness and color to your winter table.

SERVES	TOTAL TIME: 25 MINUTES	DIETARY
4 to 6	Prep Time: 10 minutes Sauté Time: 3 minutes Pressure Cook: 10 minutes	

INGREDIENTS

1 tablespoon oil

1 teaspoon black mustard seeds

1 tablespoon black peppercorns

1 tablespoon coriander seeds

1½ tablespoons grated fresh ginger

10 to 12 curry leaves

½ cup blanched almonds

4 medium beets, peeled and quartered

2 large carrots, peeled and cut into large pieces

1½ teaspoons salt, or to taste

INSTRUCTIONS

1. Set the Instant Pot® to Sauté mode and heat the oil. Add the black mustard seeds and wait until they crackle. Stir in the peppercorns, coriander seeds, ginger, curry leaves, and almonds and cook for 1 minute.

2. Press Cancel to turn off the Sauté mode. Stir in the beets, carrots, salt, and 4 cups of water.

3. Close the lid and set the Instant Pot® on Manual Pressure for 10 minutes. When cooking time is complete, do a Quick Pressure Release.

4. Once the pressure has released, open the lid. When the soup has cooled slightly, puree with an immersion blender and serve.

VEGETABLES
& PANEER

Vegetables are the crowning jewels of the Indian table. In a land where the cuisine originates from a sustainable agrarian perspective, it is very common for homes to grow some basic produce. Indeed, India is rooted in vegetarianism and the propensity towards balance, so vegetables must naturally serve as more than just a sidekick to the meat platter. I encourage you to find your favorite colors and flavors among vegetables, truly nature's palette. I personally find ornamental farmers market vegetables a lot of fun to work with and have introduced this concept in my recipes.

In Indian cooking, the creativity applied towards cooking vegetables is quite fascinating, making this a wonderful option if you are looking to broaden your vegetarian or vegan choices. Vegetables are mixed and melded in various exciting combinations, ranging from imaginative to just plain frugal ways to use up leftover bits and pieces, such as in the Labra Tarkari from Assam (page 124), and rich, sensuous dishes like the Benrasi Alu Dum (page 126), one of my favorite party offerings.

Bits of lentils and the white Indian Paneer cheese are often cooked alongside vegetables to boost their nutritional value. Paneer can be made very easily in the Instant Pot®, following the process outlined on page 26.

As with all other recipes in this book, made-head or readymade sauces can cut down your cooking time significantly, allowing you to have food on your table in minutes.

With regard to cooking vegetables using the Instant Pot®, it is important to understand that vegetables release a lot of natural water and the Instant Pot® actually senses and takes this into account. It is not necessary to add a lot of extra water—in fact doing that will just leave you with the task of having to cook down and absorb all the unnecessary additional water after the fact. Also note that vegetables do not need a lot of cooking time in the Instant Pot®. You will be amazed at how quickly they cook up. The Low Pressure and Steam settings will become your friends. In general, larger pieces of vegetables work better in the Instant Pot®. Once you get used to cutting larger pieces, you may find it quite liberating. In general, Indians tend to like their vegetables soft and tender and cooking curries in the Instant Pot® offers you these results.

OVERALL TEMPERATURE RECOMMENDATIONS FOR VEGETABLES:
While many Instant Pot® recipes call for steaming vegetables, this is actually not the typical cooking recommendation for Indian-style vegetables. We like our vegetables well done, but not mushy. To accomplish

this, most recipes suggest 0 to 2 minutes of low pressure cooking and the pressure release time varies. (Yes, there is a 0 minutes cook time!)

ADDING WATER WHILE COOKING VEGETABLES IN THE INSTANT POT®:
Most of my vegetable recipes use very little added water because the vegetables release a lot of liquid, and this works to build the steam for cooking in the Instant Pot®. Some people are surprised when they see the amount of water used—depending on the vegetable, I sometimes add no water. If you have a Duo or Ultra Model Instant Pot® I have noticed that they are more sensitive to "sensing" water in the vegetables and you might need to add a little more water than some of these recipes suggest. If, however, your Instant Pot® registers a "Burn" message, Quick Release the pressure, open the lid, and stir the food, adding water about a tablespoon at a time to let it sense the water. Believe me, this will work.

Pav Bhaji
Mixed Vegetable Paté

___

Pav Bhaji is a signature street food from Mumbai, that is usually made with a variety of vegetables and spices simmered for a long time, then mashed to a smooth consistency, slathered with butter, and served with lightly toasted, buttered rolls known as pav. *Traditionally the pav is either served on the side, or the puree is served over the bread, much like a vegan Sloppy Joe. In fact the pav is omnipresent in Mumbai, featuring on the side of an assortment of dishes. I adapted this recipe for the Instant Pot® and at the same time, reduced a lot of the unnecessary butter. We enjoy this with whole wheat hamburger rolls in place of the pav. It makes for a great nutritious refrigerator-clearing dish! Some variations of the recipe use added color, I have used Kashmiri red chili powder which provides the color without the heat.*

SERVES	TOTAL TIME: 35 MINUTES	DIETARY
4 to 6	Prep Time: 6 minutes Sauté Time: 12 minutes / 3 minutes Pressure Cook: 5 minutes Pressure Release: 5 minutes	

INGREDIENTS

3 tablespoons grapeseed oil

1 teaspoon cumin seeds

1 tablespoon grated fresh ginger

1 medium onion, chopped

4 tomatoes, chopped

1½ teaspoons ground cumin

2 teaspoons Kashmiri red chili powder

1 tablespoon dried mango powder (amchur powder)

½ medium head (about 1 pound) cauliflower, coarsely chopped

INSTRUCTIONS

1. Set the Instant Pot® to Sauté mode and heat the grapeseed oil for 1 minute. Add the cumin seeds and sauté until they crackle. Add the ginger and onion and sauté well for about 4 to 5 minutes. Add the tomatoes and cook for 2 to 3 minutes until the tomatoes soften.

2. Add the cumin, Kashmiri red chili powder, and dried mango powder and mix well. Add the cauliflower, potato, carrots, eggplant (if using), half the bell pepper, and the salt and stir well. Stir in ½ cup of water.

3. Press Cancel to turn off the Sauté mode. Close the lid, and set the Instant Pot® on Manual Pressure mode for 5 minutes.

1 large potato, peeled and quartered

2 carrots, peeled and chopped

1 medium eggplant, coarsely chopped (optional)

1 medium bell pepper, seeded, chopped

1½ teaspoons salt, or to taste

½ cup frozen green peas

1 teaspoon garam masala (page 31 or store-bought)

1 tablespoon unsalted butter

¼ cup chopped cilantro

Garnishes

Chopped red onions

Butter, if desired

Lime or lemon wedges

Whole wheat rolls or Indian-style pav bread, lightly toasted

4. When the cooking time is complete, allow for Natural Pressure Release for 5 minutes and then do a Quick Release for any residual pressure.

5. Once the pressure is released, open the lid and mash the mixture with the back of a spoon until fairly smooth.

6. Set the Instant Pot® on Sauté mode again and stir in the remaining bell pepper and green peas and allow the mixture to cook for 3 minutes or so (this allows the puree to tighten and develop the right consistency).

7. Stir in the garam masala, butter, and cilantro. Serve with chopped onions, additional butter (if desired), lime or lemon wedges, and the lightly toasted buns.

Phoolgobi Moghlai
Whole Baked Cauliflower in Tomato Mint Sauce

Phoolgobi Moghlai, in the Mughal style of cooking from North India, is a rich and multilayered dish. It is traditionally made by first lightly steaming a whole cauliflower and then slathering on the rich makhani-based sauce enhanced with herbs, nuts, and dried fruits, and then baking it until fork tender, and finishing it with a few minutes under the broiler. The whole cauliflower makes for an impressive presentation. You can achieve all this using my Basic Makhani Masala and four minutes of Instant Pot® cooking. If you want you can still finish with a few minutes of broiling, but, honestly I usually end up skipping that step and the dish still works out just fine.

SERVES	TOTAL TIME: 20 MINUTES	DIETARY
4 to 6	Prep Time: 5 minutes (not including making Makhani Masala) Sauté Time: 7 minutes Pressure Cook (Low): 3 minutes Pressure Release: 5 minutes	

INGREDIENTS

2 tablespoons grapeseed oil

1 onion, thinly sliced

¼ cup sliced cashews

1 tablespoon raisins

1 tablespoon mint powder

1 cup Basic Makhani Masala (page 30)

1 head cauliflower (2½ to 3 pounds)

2 tablespoons fresh lemon juice

1 tablespoon chopped cilantro

1 tablespoon chopped mint

INSTRUCTIONS

1. Set the Instant Pot® on Sauté mode and heat the oil. When hot, add the onion and sauté lightly for about 5 minutes. Add the cashews and raisins and cook for another minute or so. Stir in the mint powder, Basic Makhani Masala, and ¼ cup of water. Press Cancel to turn off the Sauté mode. Transfer the sauce to a bowl.

2. Carefully remove the cauliflower from its outer leaves, in a single piece. Place the whole cauliflower in the Instant Pot®. Spoon the prepared sauce over the cauliflower. Close the lid and set the Instant Pot® on Manual Low Pressure mode for 3 minutes.

3. When the cooking time is complete, allow for a Natural Pressure Release for 5 minutes.

4. Once the pressure is released, carefully remove the whole cauliflower without breaking it and place it on a serving tray or bowl. Spoon all the cooking sauce over the cauliflower. Sprinkle with lemon juice and garnish with chopped cilantro and mint.

Kobichi Bhaji
Cabbage with Split Peas

This delicate and super-quick cabbage dish from the western state of Maharastra (also known as the "5-Minute Cabbage" in our house) is a very easy and satisfying way to enjoy this vegetable. You do need to remember to soak the split peas, but be sure to use them. In addition to boosting the protein content of this dish, they add a nice texture. Cabbage is a very hardy vegetable and can be kept pre-chopped in the refrigerator for up to a week.

SERVES

4 to 6

TOTAL TIME: 10 MINUTES (plus few hours soaking time for split peas)
Prep Time: 5 minutes
Sauté Time: 3 minutes
Pressure Cook (Low): 0 minutes

DIETARY

INGREDIENTS

2 tablespoons grapeseed oil

¾ teaspoon black mustard seeds

4 to 6 curry leaves

2 whole dried red chilies

1 tablespoon grated fresh ginger

¼ teaspoon asafoetida

½ teaspoon cayenne pepper powder

½ teaspoon ground turmeric

½ cup split peas, soaked for several hours, drained

3 to 4 cups finely shredded green cabbage

2 tablespoons desiccated coconut (optional)

1 teaspoon salt

1 tablespoon chopped cilantro

INSTRUCTIONS

1. Set the Instant Pot® to Sauté mode and heat the grapeseed oil for about 1 minute. Add the mustard seeds and wait until the seeds begin to crackle. Add the curry leaves, dried red chilies, and ginger and stir well. Add the asafoetida, cayenne pepper powder, turmeric, and split peas and stir well. Stir in about 1 tablespoon of water.

2. Press Cancel to turn off Sauté mode. Add the cabbage, coconut, if using, and salt and mix well. Close the lid and set the Instant Pot® on Manual Low Pressure mode for 0 minutes. When the cook time is complete, do a Quick Pressure Release.

3. Serve hot or at room temperature as a salad, garnished with the cilantro.

Labra Tarkari
Assamese Vegetable Medley

———

Labra is an example of how dishes retain some similarities across neighboring states, but have varying spices and flavors. Labra is a mixed vegetable medley made in the states of West Bengal and Assam. The Assamese variation is more of an autumn dish, while in West Bengal the labra surfaces in early spring. The recipe offered here is the Assamese labra which uses more assertive spices, such as garlic and garam masala. Essential vegetables for this dish include pumpkin or winter squash, eggplant, and spinach. I often add some radishes into the mix and you can certainly add in anything else that you prefer.

SERVES	TOTAL TIME: 15 MINUTES	DIETARY
4 to 6	Prep Time: 6 minutes Sauté Time: 6 minutes Pressure Cook (Low): 2 minutes	

INGREDIENTS

2 tablespoons mustard oil

1 small onion, grated

2 cloves garlic minced

1 tablespoon grated fresh ginger

1 teaspoon ground cumin

1½ teaspoons garam masala
(page 31 or storebought)

1½ teaspoons salt, or to taste

1 teaspoon sugar

½ teaspoon cayenne pepper
powder

1½ cups pumpkin or winter
squash, cut into large cubes

1 medium potato, quartered

8 to 10 radishes, halved

1 small eggplant, cut into cubes

1½ cups baby spinach leaves

To finish

1 teaspoon ghee (page 27)

1 teaspoon panch phoron
(Bengali Five Spice Blend)

2 bay leaves

INSTRUCTIONS

1. Set the Instant Pot® to Sauté mode and heat the mustard oil for 1 minute. Add the onion, garlic, and ginger and cook for 3 to 4 minutes.

2. Add the cumin, garam masala, salt, sugar, and cayenne pepper powder and mix well. Stir in the pumpkin, potato, radishes, eggplant, and ½ cup of water.

3. Press Cancel to turn off the Sauté mode. Close the lid and set the Instant Pot® on Manual Low Pressure mode for 2 minutes. When cooking time is complete, do a Quick Pressure Release.

4. Once the pressure is released, remove the lid and stir in the baby spinach, allowing it to wilt. Place mixture in a serving bowl.

5. To finish, in a skillet heat the ghee, add the panch phoron, and wait until it crackles. Add the bay leaves and after a few seconds pour the ghee mixture over the labra. Serve with rice or your favorite flatbreads.

Benarasi Alu Dum
Whole Baby Potatoes with Creamy Almond Sauce

Whole baby potatoes cooked in a rich gravy to soft and tender perfection is known as Alu Dum. There is, however, no one Alu Dum across the expanse of this wide and diverse country. The Bengali variety in eastern India is spicy with a touch of sweetness. In Kashmir it is redolent with Kashmiri red chilies, and this recipe is one of the ways it is cooked in Benares. I lightened the recipe quite a bit by eliminating a lot of the deep frying. This allows the innate delicate richness of the sauce to shine.

SERVES	TOTAL TIME: 25 MINUTES	DIETARY
4 to 6	Prep Time: 5 minutes Sauté Time: 4 minutes Pressure Cook: 3 minutes Pressure Release: 10 minutes	

INGREDIENTS

For almond sauce:

½ cup light sour cream

½ cup blanched almonds

1 teaspoon garam masala (page 31 or storebought)

1 teaspoon dried fenugreek leaves (kasuri methi)

1 teaspoon salt

For potatoes:

2 tablespoons oil

1 teaspoon ground fennel

1 teaspoon ground cumin

1 tablespoon grated fresh ginger

2 whole dried red chilies

½ cup tomato sauce or fresh tomato puree

15 whole baby potatoes, peeled

INSTRUCTIONS

Prepare almond sauce:

1. Place the sour cream, almonds, garam masala, dried fenugreek leaves, and salt in a blender and blend until smooth. Set aside.

Prepare potatoes:

2. Set the Instant Pot® on Sauté mode and heat the oil. Add the fennel, cumin, and ginger and sauté for a few seconds. Add the dried red chilies, tomato sauce, and ½ cup of water. Bring to a simmer and then press Cancel to turn off the heat. Add the potatoes and almond sauce to the pot and stir.

3. Close the lid and set the Instant Pot® on Manual Pressure mode for 3 minutes. When the cooking time is complete, allow for a Natural Pressure Release for about 10 minutes. Enjoy with your favorite flatbread.

Baigan Bhartha
Mashed Eggplant with Red Onions and Chilies

———————

Baigan Bhartha, or any other bhartha, is about vegetables roasted on an open flame to char the outer skin and then peeled and mashed with a few essential spices, raw onions, and green chilies. This yields a smoky, light-tasting dish. Though the Instant Pot® will not give you that smoky taste, you will get a very flavorful, fuss-free eggplant dish that is a good busy weeknight alternative. This version also makes a great dip served with warm flatbreads.

SERVES	TOTAL TIME: 25 MINUTES	DIETARY
4 to 6	Prep Time: 3 minutes Sauté Time: 15 minutes Pressure Cook: 4 minutes	

INGREDIENTS

6 small to medium Japanese or other young eggplants

½ cup mustard oil or olive oil

6 cloves garlic, minced

1½ teaspoons ground cumin

1½ teaspoons salt, or to taste

4 tomatoes, chopped

1 red onion, minced

3 green chilies, minced

¼ cup chopped cilantro

2 tablespoons fresh lime juice

INSTRUCTIONS

1. Partially peel the eggplants lengthwise leaving some of the skin on. Cut each into 3 or 4 lengthwise pieces.

2. Set the Instant Pot® on Sauté mode and pour in ¼ cup of the oil. After a minute, carefully place about half of the eggplant pieces at the bottom of the pot in a single layer. Cook the pieces for about 3 minutes on each side and then remove to a plate. Reserving 2 tablespoons, add the remaining oil to the pot, and cook the second batch of eggplant. Remove to the plate.

3. Add the reserved 2 tablespoons of oil to the Instant Pot®. Add the garlic and cook until fragrant and slightly golden. Stir in the cumin, salt, tomatoes, and cooked eggplant.

4. Press Cancel to turn off the Sauté mode. Close the lid and set the Instant Pot® on Manual Pressure Cook for 4 minutes. When cooking time is complete, do a Quick Pressure Release.

5. Once the pressure is released, remove the lid and mash the eggplants, cooking down any liquid if necessary on Sauté mode. Stir in the raw onions, green chilies, and cilantro. Place in a serving bowl, sprinkle with the lime juice, and serve hot.

Spaghetti Squash Poriyal
South Indian Stir-Fried Spaghetti Squash

If you like spaghetti squash, you are in for a treat once you discover how to cook it in the Instant Pot®. It makes the entire process ridiculously simple. A poriyal is a stir-fry from Southern India. You can make this dish with any vegetable that suits your fancy, but the naturally delicate texture of the spaghetti squash lends itself well to stir-frying. This dish is great any time of year, but fits especially well on an autumn holiday table.

SERVES	TOTAL TIME: 25 MINUTES	DIETARY
6	Prep Time: 5 minutes Pressure Cook: 6 minutes Pressure Release: 5 minutes Sauté Time: 6 minutes	

INGREDIENTS

1 small to medium spaghetti squash (about 3 pounds)

2 tablespoons coconut oil

1 teaspoon mustard seeds

¼ teaspoon asafoetida

2 to 3 whole dried red chilies

2 shallots, thinly sliced

1 tablespoon grated fresh ginger

10 to 12 curry leaves

½ teaspoon ground turmeric

½ teaspoon cayenne pepper powder

1½ teaspoons salt, or to taste

¼ cup chopped pistachios

2 tablespoons dried cranberries (optional)

2 tablespoons fresh lime juice

> *Note:*
>
> Beets are another favorite vegetable I use for this recipe.

INSTRUCTIONS

1. Pour 1 cup of water into the Instant Pot®. Place the trivet that comes with the Instant Pot® over the water and put the squash on the trivet. Close the lid and set the Instant Pot® on Manual Pressure Cook for 6 minutes. When cooking time is complete, allow for 5 minutes of Natural Pressure Release, then use Quick Release for any residual pressure.

2. Once the pressure is released, remove the squash from the pot. When squash is cooled, cut it in half, remove the seeds, and gently scoop out the flesh and set aside.

3. In a large wok or the Instant Pot® on Sauté mode, heat the coconut oil. Add the mustard seeds, and wait until they begin to crackle. Add the asafoetida, dried red chilies, and shallots, and cook for a few seconds. Add the ginger, curry leaves, and squash and stir well. Add the turmeric, cayenne pepper powder, and salt and stir well.

4. Close the lid and let simmer for 2 more minutes. Remove the lid, mix in the pistachios, cranberries, and fresh lime juice and serve.

Alu Gobi
Curried Cauliflower and Potatoes

Pairing cauliflower and potatoes is a very common thing in the Indian kitchen. I personally find cauliflower to be a very adaptable and versatile vegetable. There are variations of this combination all across India, but this particular recipe uses basic spices from the Punjabi pantry. For the dish to work, the cauliflower should be cut in larger pieces and the potatoes in smaller cubes.

SERVES

4 to 6

TOTAL TIME: 10 MINUTES (if using pre-made Masala Paste)

Prep Time: 4 minutes
Sauté Time: 6 minutes
Pressure Cook (Low): 1 minutes

DIETARY

INGREDIENTS

1 tablespoon canola or olive oil

1 teaspoon cumin seeds

1 cup Everyday Masala Paste (page 29)

1 medium cauliflower, cut into large pieces

1 medium to large potato, peeled and cut into eighths

½ teaspoon cayenne pepper powder

½ cup frozen green peas

½ teaspoon garam masala (page 31 or storebought)

1 tablespoon chopped cilantro

INSTRUCTIONS

1. Set the Instant Pot® on Sauté mode and heat the oil. Add the cumin seeds and cook until they sizzle. Add the Everyday Masala Paste, cauliflower, and potatoes and stir well. Add the cayenne pepper powder and ¼ cup of water.

2. Press Cancel to turn off the Sauté mode. Close the lid and set the Instant Pot® on Manual Low Pressure mode for 1 minutes.

3. When cooking time is complete, do a Quick Pressure Release.

4. Once the pressure is released, open the lid and set to Sauté mode again. Add the peas and cook down any excess water. Put the Alu Gobi in a serving bowl, sprinkle with the garam masala and cilantro and enjoy.

Alu Sem

Stir-Fried Potatoes with Green Beans

This dish is a wholesome basic stir-fry found all over India. The particular flavors and sesame finish in this recipe are gathered from northeast India. Using the Sauté mode with tight sealed manual cooking, this gets done softer and quicker than on the stove-top. It puts summer beans to good use.

SERVES

4 to 6

TOTAL TIME: 20 MINUTES
Prep Time: 10 minutes
Sauté Time: 6 minutes
Pressure Cook (Low): 1 minute

DIETARY

INGREDIENTS

2 tablespoons canola or grapeseed oil

1 teaspoon cumin seeds

1 medium onion, chopped

2 cloves garlic, minced

1 tomato, chopped

2 medium potatoes, peeled and cubed

1 pound green beans, trimmed and cut into 1-inch pieces

½ teaspoon ground turmeric

½ teaspoon cayenne pepper powder

1 teaspoon salt, or to taste

1 tablespoon sesame seeds

INSTRUCTIONS

1. Set the Instant Pot® to the Sauté mode and heat the oil. Add the cumin seeds and wait until the cumin seeds begin to sizzle. Add the onion and garlic and cook briefly for a few minutes, until the onion softens and turns translucent.

2. Add the tomato and potato and mix well. Stir in the green beans, turmeric, cayenne pepper powder, salt and 2 tablespoons of water.

3. Press Cancel to turn off the Sauté mode. Close the lid and set the Instant Pot® on Manual Low Pressure for 1 minute.

4. When cooking time is complete, do a Quick Pressure Release. Open the lid, remove the vegetables from the Instant Pot®, and sprinkle with the sesame seeds before serving.

Chial Meh
Northeastern Mixed Vegetable Stir-Fry

This Chial Meh stir-fry is an adaptation of the original recipe from northeastern India, which uses similar seasoning but is a soup. I find this a perfect medley that compliments most dishes. Chinese influences spill over into the flavors of northeastern India, as can be seen with this dish.

SERVES

4 to 6

TOTAL TIME: 15 MINUTES
Prep Time: 6 minutes
Sauté Time: 2 minutes
Pressure Cook (Low): 0 minutes
Pressure Release: 5 minutes

DIETARY

INGREDIENTS

1 tablespoon oil

1 teaspoon cumin seeds

1 tablespoon minced garlic

1 tablespoon grated fresh ginger

3 cups large broccoli pieces

1 tablespoon soy sauce (or use tamari to keep dish vegan)

1 tablespoon chili garlic sauce (such as Sriracha)

1 medium red onion, cut into eighths and layers separated

1 medium carrot, peeled and cut into large pieces

1 cup sliced button or cremini mushrooms

Chopped cilantro to garnish

INSTRUCTIONS

1. Set the Instant Pot® on the Sauté mode and heat the oil. Add the cumin seeds and wait until they sizzle. Add the garlic and ginger and stir lightly. Add the broccoli, soy sauce, and chili garlic sauce and mix well.

2. Press Cancel to turn off the Sauté mode. Stir in the onion, carrot, and mushrooms.

3. Close the lid and set the Instant Pot® on Manual Low Pressure for 0 minutes.

4. When the cooking time is complete, allow for Natural Pressure Release for 5 minutes, then use Quick Release for any residual pressure. Mix well and garnish with cilantro to serve.

Note:
Using rainbow carrots would give this dish, and others, a very pretty appearance

Gajar Methi Mattar
Carrots with Fenugreek Leaves and Green Peas

This combination of fresh sweet carrots and bitter greens is another classic from the North Indian and Punjabi table. Depending on where you live you will either find fresh fenugreek leaves or you will certainly find good quality frozen fenugreek leaves at your Indian grocer. Alternately, you can use fresh kale leaves and some dried fenugreek leaves. The only real effort of time needed in cooking this dish is chopping the carrots.

SERVES

4 to 6

TOTAL TIME: 10 MINUTES
Prep Time: 5 minutes
Sauté Time: 4 minutes
Pressure Cook: 1 minute

DIETARY

INGREDIENTS

1 tablespoons oil

1 teaspoon cumin seeds

½ teaspoon ground coriander

½ teaspoon cayenne pepper powder

1 tablespoon minced fresh ginger

2 cups diced carrots

2 cups chopped fresh or frozen fenugreek leaves

½ cup green peas (can be frozen)

1 teaspoon salt

1 teaspoon garam masala (page 31 or storebought)

2 tablespoons fresh lime juice

INSTRUCTIONS

1. Set the Instant Pot® on Sauté mode and heat the oil for 1 minute. Add the cumin seeds and wait until the seeds begin to crackle. Add the coriander, cayenne pepper powder, ginger, and carrots and sauté well. Add the fenugreek leaves, green peas, and salt and mix well.

2. Press Cancel to turn off the Sauté mode, close the lid, and set the Instant Pot® on Manual Pressure for 1 minute.

3. When cooking time is complete, do a Quick Pressure Release. Stir well. Stir in the garam masala and fresh lime juice and serve hot.

Bhindi Masala Subji
Stir-Fried Okra with Onions and Tomatoes

Cooking okra in the Instant Pot® takes a little leap of faith and some encouragement from mom. I have always been reserved about doing anything that resembles steaming where okra is concerned. My mom assured me, however, that all would be well as long as I made sure the okra was prepped and chopped, and that there was no extra water. Saying silent prayers to the okra gods, I developed this recipe that has flavors from Madhya Pradesh, the central heartland of India.

SERVES	TOTAL TIME: 25 MINUTES	DIETARY
4 to 6	Prep Time: 5 minutes Sauté Time: 9 minutes Pressure Cook (Low): 1 minute	

INGREDIENTS

2 tablespoons mustard oil (or other oil)

1 teaspoon cumin seeds

1 large onion, thinly sliced

1 tablespoon grated fresh ginger

2 tomatoes, minced

1½ pounds fresh young okra, trimmed and cut into ½-inch pieces

1 teaspoon salt

1 teaspoon cayenne pepper powder

1 teaspoon dried mango powder (amchur powder) or 2 tablespoons fresh lime juice

1 tablespoon chopped cilantro

INSTRUCTIONS

1. Set the Instant Pot® on medium Sauté mode. Heat the oil for about 1 minute. Add the cumin seeds and when the seeds sizzle, add the onion and sauté for about 5 minutes.

2. Add the ginger and sauté for a few seconds. Add the tomatoes and cook for 2 minutes. Stir in the okra, salt, cayenne pepper powder, and mango powder or lime juice.

3. Press Cancel to turn off the Sauté mode, close the lid, and set the Instant Pot® on Manual Low Pressure for 1 minute.

4. When cooking time is complete, do a Quick Pressure Release. Garnish with cilantro before serving.

Channar Dalna
Paneer with Potatoes and Green Peas in Fragrant Coconut Sauce

---

This particular recipe is a hack of a classic Bengali recipe. The traditional recipe requires hours of slow cooking the onions to reach a caramelized golden consistency. Using my Everyday Masala Paste, I developed a quicker variation that will do on short notice. If you wish to substitute sweet potatoes for the potatoes, that works well in this recipe.

SERVES

4 to 6

TOTAL TIME: 30 MINUTES
Prep Time: 5 minutes
Sauté Time: 10 minutes
Pressure Cook (Low): 2 minutes
Pressure Release: 10 minutes

DIETARY

INGREDIENTS

2 tablespoons grapeseed oil

1 or 2 bay leaves

1 small cinnamon stick

2 medium potatoes, peeled and cut into cubes

½ cup Everyday Masala Paste (page 29)

2 tablespoons plain yogurt

½ cup thick coconut milk

1 teaspoon salt, or to taste

½ teaspoon cayenne pepper powder

1½ teaspoons sugar

1 cup green peas

1 recipe homemade paneer, cubed (page 26)

INSTRUCTIONS

1. Set the Instant Pot® to Sauté mode and heat the grapeseed oil. Add the bay leaves and cinnamon stick and sizzle for a few seconds. Add the potatoes and stir well until they are well coated.

2. Stir in the Everyday Masala Paste and yogurt and bring to a simmer. Stir in the coconut milk, salt, cayenne pepper powder, sugar, green peas, and paneer.

3. Press Cancel to turn off the Sauté mode. Close the lid and set the Instant Pot® on Manual Low Pressure for 2 minutes. When the cooking time is complete, allow for a Natural Pressure Release for about 10 minutes. Enjoy with steamed white rice.

Saag Paneer/Tofu
Creamy Spinach with Paneer/Tofu

Saag Paneer is a soulful, homestyle dish, particularly favored on winter tables in India. There are many ways of making this dish and this particular recipe is something that I tasted in a small homey restaurant in the mountain regions of Uttarkhand. My vegetarian daughter is especially fond of it. She won't eat it with paneer, but she does like the vegan version made with tofu. Using frozen spinach for this recipe is a perfectly viable option, but it is important to squeeze out the excess water from the spinach before cooking.

SERVES

4 to 6

TOTAL TIME: 15 MINUTES
Prep Time: 5 minutes
Sauté Time: 5 minutes
Pressure Cook (Low): 2 minutes

DIETARY

INGREDIENTS

2 tablespoons grapeseed oil

1 teaspoon cumin seeds

1 medium onion, chopped

1 tablespoon grated fresh ginger

2 pounds freshly chopped spinach or spinach and kale

1 teaspoon salt, or to taste

1 teaspoon ground turmeric

1 teaspoon ground cumin

1 teaspoon ground coriander

2 green chilies, minced

2 tomatoes, chopped

½ cup thick coconut cream (cream or yogurt can be used as substitute)

1 cup cubed paneer (page 26) or tofu

1 teaspoon garam masala (page 31 or storebought)

1 tablespoon chopped cilantro

INSTRUCTIONS

1. Set the Instant Pot® on Sauté mode, and heat the grapeseed oil. Add the cumin seeds and cook until the seeds begin to sizzle. Add the onion and ginger and stir well.

2. Stir in the spinach, salt, turmeric, cumin, and coriander. Add the green chilies and tomatoes and cook until the spinach is wilted. Stir in the coconut cream. Press Cancel to turn off the Sauté mode.

3. Using an immersion blender, process the spinach mixture until somewhat smooth—it is important to have some texture for this dish.

4. Stir in the paneer or tofu. Close the lid and set the Instant Pot® on Manual Low Pressure for 2 minutes. When cooking time is complete, do a Quick Pressure Release.

5. Once the pressure is released, remove the lid, stir in the garam masala and cilantro, and serve with homemade or storebought flatbreads.

Paneer Bhujri
Stir-Fried Paneer with Bell Peppers

A light, fresh cheese dish, Paneer Bhujri is the vegetarian answer to scrambled eggs. The dish originates from Punjab, known for its fresh dairy products. To make this vegan, you can use soft tofu instead of the fresh paneer. The paneer used in this dish is freshly made following the instructions on page 26, and then drained lightly. No pressing is needed.

SERVES

4 to 6

TOTAL TIME: 10 MINUTES
Prep Time: 5 minutes (plus 2 to 4 hours for making paneer)
Sauté Time: 3 minutes
Pressure Cook (Low): 0 minute

DIETARY

INGREDIENTS

2 tablespoons oil

1 teaspoon cumin seeds

1 red onion, chopped

1 tablespoon grated fresh ginger

½ medium red bell pepper, chopped

½ medium green bell pepper, chopped

¼ teaspoon ground turmeric

2 green chilies, minced

1 cup freshly-made paneer curds (page 26)

1 tomato, chopped

1 teaspoon salt or to taste

1 tablespoon lime juice

2 tablespoons chopped cilantro

INSTRUCTIONS

1. Set the Instant Pot® to Sauté mode and heat the oil. After about 30 seconds, add the cumin seeds and cook until they begin to sizzle. Add the onion and ginger and sauté until the onion softens. Add the red bell pepper and green bell pepper and stir. Add the turmeric, green chilies, paneer curds, tomato, and salt and mix well.

2. Press Cancel to turn off the Sauté mode. Close the lid, and set the Instant Pot® on Manual Low Pressure for 0 minute.

3. When cooking time is complete, do a Quick Pressure Release. Once the pressure is released, open the pot and stir well. Stir in the lime juice and cilantro and serve.

FISH & SHRIMP

On the coast and alongside the rivers Hoogly, Yamuna, and Kaveri fish rules. You will find a very creative assortment of dishes, particularly using shellfish, right alongside the regular fish. If you visit the beaches of India, it is not unusual to find street vendors grilling and selling their catch of the day. A perfect example of cooking and eating close to the source! This chapter includes some of my favorite essential seafood recipes, ones that I have simplified and served up countless times on weeknights and festive occasions alike.

Cooking fish in the Instant Pot® can take a little getting used to. In truth, it is not very different from cooking vegetables, in that a delicate touch is preferred. One of the things that you can do without batting an eyelid is use frozen fish unthawed for making the curries. I have found it helpful to cut up and divide fish into portions, and then freeze the appropriately sized portions in zip-top bags. This way you can just add the contents of the bag to the sauce and you are usually ready to eat in well under 30 minutes.

Macchi Poodina Korma
Fish in Creamy Tomato Mint Sauce

Kormas are creamy, relatively mild creations from the Mughal cuisine of northern India. The korma sauce offers a delicate touch from ground nuts and cream. I like to use salmon for this dish, but any variety of firm-fleshed fish would work. This recipe uses a ridiculously simple approach to get amazing results. The finish with the fresh mint adds a nice perkiness to the dish.

SERVES	TOTAL TIME: 15 MINUTES	DIETARY
4 to 6	Prep Time: 5 minutes Pressure Cook (Low): 3 minutes	

INGREDIENTS

½ cup raw blanched almonds

¼ cup heavy cream

1 cup Everyday Masala Paste (page 29)

1½ pounds fresh or frozen fish fillets (such as salmon), cubed

½ cup chopped fresh mint

INSTRUCTIONS

1. Place the blanched almonds and heavy cream in a blender and blend until smooth. Add masala paste and blend until smooth. Pour into the Instant Pot®.

2. Place the fish in the Instant Pot® and toss to coat with the sauce. Close the lid and set the Instant Pot® on Manual Low Pressure for 3 minutes.

3. When cooking time is complete, do a Quick Pressure Release. Remove the cover and stir well. Stir in the mint leaves and serve.

Patra Ni Macchi
Steamed Fish with Coconut and Herb Chutney

This delicate fish preparation is another offering from the Parsee community. Here fish is slathered with a fresh coconut, cilantro, and mint chutney, wrapped in banana leaves and then steamed. Each diner is usually given an individually wrapped package to unwrap and savor. Now, one of the things I have done with this recipe is to simplify the process of individual wrapping, which I have found takes a lot of time. Instead I line the steaming basket with banana leaves to infuse the flavor and steam the fish in the prepared fresh sauce.

SERVES	**TOTAL TIME: 35 MINUTES**	**DIETARY**
4 to 6	Prep Time: 15 minutes Steam Time: 7 minutes Pressure Release: 10 minutes	

INGREDIENTS

1 cup flaked or chopped coconut

3 green chilies

1 cup chopped cilantro

½ cup chopped fresh mint

1 (2-inch) piece ginger, peeled

3 cloves garlic

1½ teaspoons salt, or to taste

¼ cup fresh lime or lemon juice

2 tablespoons oil

6 pompano steaks or any firm-fleshed fish fillets (about 2 pounds)

Banana leaves or parchment paper

Red pepper flakes to garnish, optional

INSTRUCTIONS

1. Place the coconut, green chilies, cilantro, mint, ginger, garlic, salt, lime juice, and oil in a blender. Blend to make a smooth, pesto-like masala sauce, adding a little water if needed.

2. Prepare the steaming pan by first adding a large piece of parchment paper and a piece of banana leaf at the base (the banana leaf is optional, but it adds flavor). Place the fish on top of the banana leaf and slather generously with the green masala sauce. Cover with another large piece of parchment paper.

3. Pour 2 cups of water into the Instant Pot®. Place a trivet in the Instant Pot® and then place the steaming pan with the fish over the trivet. Close the lid, and set the Instant Pot® to Steam mode for 7 minutes.

4. When the cooking time is complete, allow for Natural Pressure Release for 10 minutes, then use Quick Release for any residual pressure. Open the lid, and carefully remove the fish. Serve immediately with plain rice or Parsee Brown Rice (page 65).

Macher Jhol

Coconut Fish Curry with Cauliflower and Eggplant

———

This beautiful Bengali fish curry is one of my favorite, fail-safe dishes. I make it on weeknights for the family, and on weekends for a crowd as well. It is flexible—sometimes I use just the squash, other times just the potatoes, and when able, of course, I use both.

I tried this recipe in the pressure cooker on a very busy evening, using frozen fish steaks to boot. In twenty minutes, I had a perfectly cooked fish stew on the table! Now I cannot imagine any other way of doing it. Traditionally pomfret or pompano steaks are used for this dish. I tend to use halibut, but you can use any firm white fish of your choice. I have had good results with sea bass and cod. The only caveat here is to choose somewhat thick, firm fish fillets. The fillets can be frozen and there is no need to defrost the fish before cooking.

SERVES	TOTAL TIME: 30 MINUTES	DIETARY
4 to 6	Prep Time: 10 minutes Sauté Time: 10 minutes Pressure Cook (Low): 2 minutes Pressure Release: 5 minutes	

INGREDIENTS

1½ pounds halibut fillets or steaks (can be frozen)

1½ teaspoons ground turmeric

1½ teaspoons salt, or to taste

3 tablespoons coconut oil or olive oil

1½ teaspoons nigella seeds

1 medium red onion, minced

1 tablespoon grated fresh ginger

½ pound winter squash (such as a kabocha), peeled and cubed

1 medium potato, peeled and quartered

1 small eggplant, cut into wedges

1 pound cauliflower, cut into medium florets

1 tomato, finely chopped (optional)

2 green serrano chilies, minced

½ cup coconut milk

1 tablespoon chopped cilantro

1 tablespoon fresh lime juice (optional)

INSTRUCTIONS

1. Cut the fish into 2- to 3-inch pieces. Place the fish in a mixing bowl, toss with half the turmeric and half the salt, and set aside as you continue with the rest of the prep.

2. Set the Instant Pot® on Sauté mode and heat the oil. Add the nigella seeds and wait until they begin to crackle, about 30 seconds. Add the remaining turmeric, remaining salt, and the onion and ginger and sauté for about 5 minutes, until the onion is soft and translucent.

3. Add the squash, potato, eggplant, and cauliflower and mix well. Add the chopped tomato, if using, and mix well and continue cooking until the tomato soften. Stir in the chilies, coconut milk, and ¼ cup of water and bring to a simmer. Add the fish.

4. Press Cancel to turn off the Sauté mode. Close the lid and set the Instant Pot® on Manual Low Pressure for 2 minutes.

5. When cooking time is complete, allow for Natural Pressure Release for 5 minutes and then use Quick Release for any residual pressure. Place in a serving bowl, garnish with cilantro and sprinkle with lime juice, if using.

Bhapa Doi Shorse Maach
Steamed Salmon with Mustard and Poppy Seeds

This steamed, mustardy salmon is a classic Bengali fish dish. Bhapa Doi Shorshe Maach is another way to celebrate our love for pairing fish with mustard. Steaming is a much-loved cooking technique in the Bengali kitchen, especially with super fresh fish. This dish is a natural for the Instant Pot®, resulting in a delicate and silky spicy sauce that is perfect over steamed rice.

SERVES

4 to 6

TOTAL TIME: 25 MINUTES
Prep Time: 10 minutes
Steam Cook: 12 minutes

DIETARY

INGREDIENTS

For mustard paste:

1 tablespoon black mustard seeds

1 tablespoon poppy seeds

1 tablespoon sliced almonds or whole cashews

½ cup plain yogurt

2 green chilies

½ teaspoon ground turmeric

1 teaspoon salt, or to taste

2 tablespoons mustard oil

For salmon and garnish:

1½ pounds wild-caught salmon fillet, cut into 2-inch pieces

2 tablespoons chopped cilantro

1 jalapeno or 2 or 3 green chilies, slit

1 tablespoon mustard oil to drizzle (optional)

INSTRUCTIONS

Prepare mustard paste:

1. Place the mustard seeds, poppy seeds, and almonds or cashews in a spice mill or coffee grinder and grind into a smooth powder. Place this powder in a blender with the yogurt, green chilies, turmeric, salt, mustard oil, and a few tablespoons of water, and blend to a paste.

Prepare salmon:

2. Place the salmon in a small glass heatproof dish (that can fit in the Instant Pot®) and pour the prepared mustard paste over it.

3. Pour about 2 cups of water into your Instant Pot®. Place a trivet over the water and place your dish with the salmon over the trivet. Close the lid and set the Instant Pot® to the Steam mode for 12 minutes.

4. When cooking time is complete, you can do a Quick Pressure Release. Remove the dish from the Instant Pot®. Garnish the salmon with cilantro and jalapeno, and drizzle with the mustard oil before serving.

Goan Fish Curry
Fish Curry with Tangy Coconut Sauce

———

Goa is a beautiful state on the southwestern coast of India. A former Portuguese colony, its cuisine incorporates strong European influences, such as the use of vinegar and garlic. This particular fish curry uses tomatoes and lime juice as souring agents. I use frozen fish for this, and highly recommend you try it as well. I personally love using salmon fillets for this recipe as I have found the stronger flavors of this dish complement the rich taste of salmon beautifully. If you work sequentially and have everything organized, this dish takes less than half an hour to finish.

SERVES	TOTAL TIME: 30 MINUTES	DIETARY
4 to 6	Prep Time: 5 minutes Sauté Time: 10 minutes Pressure Cook (Low): 2 minutes Pressure Release: 10 minutes	

INGREDIENTS

2 medium red onions, quartered

4 cloves garlic

1-inch piece fresh ginger, peeled

2 green chilies

2 teaspoons ground coriander

1½ teaspoons salt, or to taste

2 tablespoons oil

1 teaspoon mustard seeds

8 to 10 curry leaves (optional)

2 medium tomatoes, chopped

2 pounds salmon fillets, cubed (frozen works fine)

½ cup coconut milk

2 tablespoons fresh lime juice

Chopped cilantro to garnish (optional)

INSTRUCTIONS

1. Place the onions, garlic, ginger, green chilies, and coriander in a food processor or chopper and process until finely chopped.

2. Set the Instant Pot® to the Sauté mode. Heat the oil for a couple of minutes. Add the mustard seeds and when they crackle add the curry leaves, if using. Add the prepared onion mixture and sauté for about 3 to 4 minutes.

3. Stir in the tomatoes and cook for couple of minutes. Add the salmon cubes, coconut milk, and about ¼ cup of water.

4. Press Cancel to turn off the Sauté mode. Close the lid and set the Instant Pot® on Manual Low Pressure for 2 minutes.

5. When the cooking time is complete, allow for Natural Pressure Release for 10 minutes, then use Quick Release for any residual pressure. Open the lid and stir in the lime juice. Remove the curry from the Instant Pot®, garnish with chopped cilantro (if desired), and serve immediately with basmati rice or Cumin-Scented Brown Rice with Green Peas (page 66).

Fish Curry with Fenugreek

This recipe from Northern India is light, flavorful, and perfect for almost any meal or event. It features on my table several times a month, prepared with mostly pantry staples. The chopped green onions are my addition to the recipe. I often have a few stalks handy in my refrigerator that I like to use in dishes like this for added flavor.

SERVES	TOTAL TIME: 20 MINUTES	DIETARY
4 to 6	Prep Time: 5 minutes Sauté Time: 5 minutes Pressure Cook (Low): 1 minute Pressure Release: 5 minutes	

INGREDIENTS

1 medium onion, chopped

4 cloves garlic, minced

3 or 4 tomatoes, chopped

2 tablespoons mustard oil or grapeseed oil

1 teaspoon cumin seeds

½ teaspoon ground turmeric

1 teaspoon cayenne pepper powder

1½ pounds cubed fresh or frozen white fish fillets (such as halibut or cod)

1 teaspoon salt

1 tablespoon dried fenugreek leaves (kasuri methi)

1 teaspoon garam masala (page 31 or storebought)

½ cup chopped green onions

INSTRUCTIONS

1. Place the onion, garlic, and tomatoes in a food processor or mini chopper and process until minced.

2. Set the Instant Pot® on Sauté mode and heat the oil. Add the cumin seeds, wait until they begin to sizzle then add the tomato mixture and sauté for 2 to 3 minutes, until it darkens a little. Stir in the turmeric, cayenne pepper powder, and ¼ cup of water, and bring to a simmer. Add the fish and salt and stir gently to coat.

3. Press Cancel to turn off the Sauté mode, close the lid, and set the Instant Pot® on Manual Low Pressure for 1 minute.

4. When the cooking time is complete, allow for Natural Pressure Release for 5 minutes and then use Quick Release for any residual pressure.

5. Remove the cover and gently stir in the dried fenugreek leaves, garam masala, and green onions. Serve hot with rice or flatbreads.

Doi Maach

Fish Poached in Fragrant Yogurt Sauce

Poached fish in a delicate yogurt sauce is a signature recipe from West Bengal. A nuanced dish like this is usually served on special occasions such as a wedding. Since we can get it done in a breeze in the Instant Pot®, it becomes perfect for any festive meal, served with something like the Misthi Pulao (Bengali Festive Golden Pilaf; on page 79).

SERVES

4 to 6

TOTAL TIME: 20 MINUTES
Prep Time: 5 minutes
Sauté Time: 4 minutes
Pressure Cook (Low): 1 minutes
Pressure Release: 5 minutes

DIETARY

INGREDIENTS

1½ pounds halibut or snapper fish fillets, cut into cubes

½ teaspoon ground turmeric

½ teaspoon cayenne pepper powder

1 teaspoon salt

¼ cup grapeseed oil

1 medium onion, grated

1 tablespoon grated fresh ginger

1 teaspoon sugar

1½ teaspoons garam masala (page 31 or storebought)

1½ cups plain yogurt, beaten

1 teaspoon ghee (page 27)

1 tablespoon raw unsalted cashews

1 tablespoon raisins

INSTRUCTIONS

1. Place the fish in a mixing bowl and toss with the turmeric, cayenne pepper powder, and salt.

2. Set the Instant Pot® on Sauté mode, and heat the oil until the pot registers hot. Add the onion and ginger and cook until the raw smell dissipates, about 2 minutes.

3. Press Cancel to turn off Sauté mode. Stir in the fish, sugar, garam masala, and ¼ cup water. Close the lid, and set the Instant Pot® on Manual Low Pressure for 1 minutes.

4. When the cooking time is complete, allow for Natural Pressure Release for 5 minutes, then use Quick Pressure Release for any residual pressure. Once the pressure is released, remove the lid and gently stir in the yogurt.

5. Heat the ghee in a small skillet and add the cashews and raisins and cook until the raisins are plump. Place the fish in a serving bowl and pour the toasted cashew-raisin mixture over it and serve.

CheMeen Kari
Kerala Shrimp Curry

This recipe is from the home kitchen of Mrs. Thomas, a family friend from Kerala who actually used to refer to it as "Bombay Curry." Upon further exploration I was rather amused to understand further details of this name. The dish is made with supposedly "new-fangled" ingredients such as tomatoes instead of tamarind, hence relegated to Bombay rather than Kerala. No matter the name, the general flavor profile is delicate and herby and makes a perfect dish with steamed rosemata rice.

SERVES	TOTAL TIME: 20 MINUTES	DIETARY
4 to 6	Prep Time: 10 minutes Sauté Time: 8 minutes Pressure Cook (Low): 2 minutes	

INGREDIENTS

2 to 3 tablespoons coconut oil

1 teaspoon mustard seeds

10 to 12 curry leaves

1 medium red onion, chopped

1 tablespoon grated fresh ginger

1½ teaspoons ground coriander

2 or 3 cardamom pods

1 (2-inch) cinnamon stick

1 teaspoon cayenne pepper powder

3 tomatoes, chopped

1½ pounds large shrimp, shelled and deveined

½ cup coconut milk

1 tablespoon chopped cilantro

INSTRUCTIONS

1. Set the Instant Pot® on Sauté mode. Heat the coconut oil until the pot registers hot. Add the mustard seeds and wait until the seeds begin to crackle. Add the curry leaves, red onion, and grated ginger, and sauté lightly for 3 to 4 minutes.

2. Stir in the coriander, cardamom pods, cinnamon stick, cayenne pepper powder, and tomatoes and cook until the tomatoes have softened. Stir in the shrimp and coconut milk.

3. Press Cancel to turn off the Sauté mode. Close the lid and set the Instant Pot® to Manual Low Pressure for 2 minutes.

4. When the cooking time is complete, do a Quick Pressure Release. Remove the cover and stir well. Put the curry in a serving bowl and garnish with the cilantro.

Chingri Tikka Masala
Shrimp in Tomato Fenugreek Sauce

———

This is another easy-breezy recipe, and uses a simpler take on the Basic Makhani Sauce (page 30) that's perfect if you are in a rush. This recipe is another signature Indian restaurant special and goes well with steamed white rice.

SERVES	TOTAL TIME: 25 MINUTES	DIETARY
4 to 6	Prep Time: 10 minutes Sauté Time: 2 minutes / 6 minutes Pressure Cook (Low): 3 minutes	

INGREDIENTS

2 tablespoons oil

4 to 6 tomatoes, chopped, or 1 cup diced canned tomatoes

1 tablespoon grated fresh ginger

4 cloves garlic, minced (about 1 tablespoon)

1 medium onion, minced

1 teaspoon cayenne pepper powder

1 teaspoon garam masala (page 31 or storebought)

1 teaspoon sugar

1 teaspoon salt

1 cup coconut milk, or ¾ cup heavy cream

1½ pounds large shrimp, shelled and deveined

¼ cup dried fenugreek leaves (kasuri methi)

Chopped cilantro for garnish

INSTRUCTIONS

1. Set the Instant Pot® to Sauté mode and heat the oil. Add the tomatoes, ginger, garlic, onion, cayenne pepper powder, garam masala, sugar, and salt. Press Cancel to turn off Sauté mode. Close the lid and set the Instant Pot® on Manual Low Pressure for 3 minutes.

2. When cooking time is complete, do Quick Pressure Release. Once the pressure is released, open the lid, stir in the coconut milk or cream, and blend sauce with an immersion blender until smooth.

4. Set the Instant Pot® on Sauté mode again. Stir in the shrimp and simmer for 5 minutes. Stir in the fenugreek leaves and simmer 30 more seconds. Serve garnished with some cilantro.

CHICKEN & EGGS

Chicken is quite the workhorse meat-based protein in our household. My husband and daughter are vegetarian, so when I am looking for a carnivorous fix, chicken is what I tend to buy. It cooks quickly, and you end up with a very flavorful result in your Instant Pot®. Luckily for us, the Indian table is brimming with incredible chicken recipes from all over the country. And as amazing as Butter Chicken is, there are many other wonderful chicken offerings in the Indian cuisine.

The key element to remember when using the Instant Pot® is that chicken and other meats contain a lot of natural moisture. We can account for this when cooking vegetables, but with chicken it is not quite so intuitive. So for the recipes in this chapter, I use minimal additional moisture to avoid ending up with a curry that has too much liquid. Allowing the chicken to release its natural juices also makes for a more flavorful curry. Everyday chicken curries on the Indian table are light and use a good balance of spices to make a flavorful meal. Most of the recipes here call for boneless chicken. I will confess, however, that the preference on the traditional Indian table is to use bone-in chicken which makes for a deeper, richer flavor, as in my recipes for Korma (page 176) and Murgh Hariali (opposite page). Chicken on the Indian table is also enjoyed without the skin. To get closer to the taste of local Indian chicken buy organic, which other than having a better taste is healthier for you as you do not have to deal with extra hormones or antibiotics that are found in processed chicken. The chicken curries freeze reasonably well and can be doubled if you wish.

Then there are eggs. Cooking eggs in the Instant Pot® is very easy. If you refer to my section on prepping ahead (page 27), you will see that one of my failsafe standbys is having some hardboiled eggs in the refrigerator. Essentially you can pop your eggs in the Instant Pot®, and they are ready in five minutes. With hardboiled eggs already on hand, most of my recipes are done in well under 30 minutes. Also, here is a secret—most of my fish and seafood recipes can be adapted for eggs. Hardboiled eggs can easily be added to most dishes to give them a protein boost. Hardboiled eggs keep well in the refrigerator for up to a week, however I would advise against freezing them—the whites tend to become stringy and do not make for a palatable offering.

Murgh Hariali
Chicken in Tomato Herb Sauce

___

This chicken curry from the central Indian heartland of Madhya Pradesh is yet another recipe made easier with the use of a readymade sauce. While this recipe uses the mild Basic Makhani Masala, the herb paste added after cooking is fairly hot due to the addition of green chilies. I add a fresh twist to this dish by adding the herb and chili mixture later to allow the intensity of the herbs to shine.

SERVES	TOTAL TIME: 20 MINUTES	DIETARY
6	Prep Time: 5 minutes (using premade masala) Pressure Cook (Low): 4 minutes Pressure Release: 5 minutes	

INGREDIENTS

1½ cups Basic Makhani Masala (page 30)

2 pounds boneless skinless chicken thighs, cut into 2-inch pieces

1 cup packed cilantro leaves

1 cup packed mint leaves

3 or 4 green chilies

2 tablespoons fresh lime juice

2 tablespoons plain yogurt

1 teaspoon salt, or to taste

photo page 166

INSTRUCTIONS

1. Place the Basic Makhani Masala and chicken pieces in the Instant Pot®. Close the lid and set the Instant Pot® on Manual Pressure for 4 minutes.

2. While the chicken is cooking, place the cilantro, mint, green chilies, lime juice, yogurt, and salt in a food processor and process until finely chopped.

3. When the cooking time is complete, allow for Natural Pressure Release for 5 minutes, followed by Quick Release of any residual pressure.

4. Once the pressure is released, open the lid and stir the chopped herb mixture sauce into the chicken. Serve immediately.

Cozy Butter Chicken
Creamy Chicken Curry with Tomato Fenugreek Sauce

———

Butter Chicken is one of those dishes that makes a party complete. A classic from the corners of old Delhi in Northern India, this dish has seen many variations, including the creation of its famous cousin, Chicken Tikka Masala. This is our household's easy variation, sure to warm us up on chilly days—which is why we call it "Cozy" Butter Chicken. It is an incredibly flavorful version of the comforting chicken dish, but without any cream. Greek yogurt yields a thick, flavorful sauce that is finished with a dollop of butter to add in the right amount of indulgence.

SERVES	TOTAL TIME: 40 MINUTES	DIETARY
4 to 6	Prep Time: 5 minutes Sauté Time: 15 minutes Pressure Cook: 10 minutes Pressure Release: 10 minutes	

INGREDIENTS

2 tablespoons oil

1 medium red onion, minced

4 cloves garlic, minced

1 tablespoon grated fresh ginger

1 tablespoon tandoori masala (page 34)

1 tablespoon Kashmiri red chili powder or paprika

½ teaspoon cayenne pepper powder

2 pounds boneless skinless chicken thighs

1 teaspoon salt, or to taste

¾ cup tomato puree

1 tablespoon tomato paste

1 teaspoon sugar

½ cup plain Greek yogurt

1 tablespoon dried fenugreek leaves (kasuri methi)

1 tablespoon fresh organic butter or ghee (page 27)

INSTRUCTIONS

1. Set the Instant Pot® to Sauté mode and heat the oil. Add the onion, garlic, and ginger and sauté for about 6 to 8 minutes, stirring well, to allow the onions to gently turn pale, golden brown.

2. Mix in the tandoori masala, Kashmiri red chili powder, cayenne pepper powder, chicken thighs, and salt and sauté for another 3 to 4 minutes, stirring often.

3. Stir in the tomato puree, tomato paste, and sugar and stir well. Add the Greek yogurt and mix well.

4. Press Cancel to turn off the Sauté mode. Close the lid and set the Instant Pot® on Manual Pressure for 10 minutes.

5. When the cooking time is complete, allow for Natural Pressure Release for 10 minutes. Once the pressure is released, remove the cover and gently stir in the fenugreek leaves and butter or ghee. Serve with bread or steamed fresh hot rice.

Adrak Saufwale Murgi
Chicken Curry with Ginger, Fennel and Thyme

I sampled this Delhi chicken curry on a vacation walking through the lanes of Old Delhi. The spicing was delicate and ever so subtle, and the technique was cooking meat on the bone low and slow. But wait, it does not stop there. This fall-off-the-bone tender meat is pulled from the bone and then dunked back into the cooking liquid. A generous dollop of thick yogurt is whipped in and you have a meal fit for a king. I've adapted this recipe using boneless chicken and added thyme for an optional interesting flavor note. Done well, this dish could give the ever-popular Butter Chicken a run for its money.

SERVES	TOTAL TIME: 35 MINUTES	DIETARY
4 to 6	Prep Time: 5 minutes Sauté Time: 8 minutes Rice Mode: 12 minutes Pressure Release: 10 minutes	

INGREDIENTS

3 tablespoons oil

1 tablespoon cumin seeds

1 tablespoon grated fresh ginger

1 medium red onion, chopped

1 tablespoon cayenne pepper powder

1 tablespoon ground fennel

2 pounds boneless skinless chicken thighs, cut into 2-inch pieces

1 teaspoon salt

1 cup full-fat plain yogurt

1½ teaspoons dried thyme (optional)

2 tablespoons chopped cilantro

INSTRUCTIONS

1. Set the Instant Pot® to Sauté mode and heat the oil. Add the cumin seeds and ginger and sauté for a few seconds. Add the onion and sauté for 6 minutes. Add the cayenne pepper powder, ground fennel, and chicken and mix well. Stir in the salt and ¼ cup water.

2. Press Cancel to turn off Sauté mode. Close the lid and set the Instant Pot® on Rice mode (12 minutes)—this setting works very well for boneless chicken.

3. When the cooking time is complete, allow for Natural Pressure Release for 10 minutes. Once the pressure is released, remove the lid. Beat the yogurt in a separate bowl and then stir into the hot chicken. Stir in the thyme, if using.

4. Taste for seasonings, place chicken on a serving dish and garnish with the cilantro. Serve hot with rice or flatbreads.

Moorgi Bhapa
Steamed Chicken with Lemon, Coconut and Basil

———

Steaming chicken or fish is common along the east and northeast of India. The meat or fish is usually wrapped in banana leaves or placed in a bamboo tray, which itself imparts a unique flavor to the food. The forests of northeastern India also offer a prolific assortment of herbs and unique spices. Inspired by the technique and flavor profiles of the region, I created this recipe with readily available ingredients.

SERVES	TOTAL TIME: 40 MINUTES	DIETARY
6	Marinate Time: 10 minutes (or up to overnight) Prep Time: 3 minutes Steam Time: 12 minutes Pressure Release: 15 minutes	

INGREDIENTS

¼ cup mustard oil

2 tablespoons grated fresh ginger

1 tablespoon chopped garlic

3 or 4 green chilies

½ cup fresh or frozen coconut

1 teaspoon ground turmeric

2 tablespoons soy sauce

2 pounds skinless boneless chicken thighs, cut into 2-inch pieces

2 tomatoes, chopped

2 tablespoons fresh lemon or Meyer lemon juice

1 teaspoon grated lemon zest

1 tablespoon chopped basil

1 tablespoon chopped cilantro

INSTRUCTIONS

1. Place the mustard oil, ginger, garlic, chilies, and coconut in a blender and blend to a paste. Place in a mixing bowl or a steamtable insert (it is great to line this with banana leaves if you have them). Add the turmeric, soy sauce, and chicken and toss to coat. Let marinate for 10 minutes or up to overnight.

2. Pour 1 cup water in the Instant Pot®. Add a trivet. Stir the tomatoes into the chicken mixture. Place the bowl with the chicken over the trivet. Close the lid and set the Instant Pot® on Steam mode for 12 minutes.

3. When cooking time is complete, allow for Natural Pressure Release for 15 minutes.

4. Once the pressure is released, open the lid and remove the container from the Instant Pot®. Stir in the lemon juice, lemon zest, basil, and cilantro. Serve over freshly steamed rice.

Saag Murgh

Mom's Chicken Curry with Seasonal Greens

———

A favorite in my mom's kitchen was a very simple rendition of chicken cooked with fresh seasonal greens and Bengali spices. It was pure, wholesome, comforting, and redolent with the rich and heady scents of cinnamon, cardamom, and ginger. I once re-created this for a casual dinner with friends. I did not have a lot of time, but I did have a lot of kale and spinach on hand. Childhood memories helped me recapture this lovely dish, almost the way mom made it. It has been an unqualified hit since.

SERVES	TOTAL TIME: 40 MINUTES	DIETARY
4 to 6	Prep Time: 10 minutes Sauté Time: 8 minutes Pressure Cook: 5 minutes Pressure Release: 10 minutes	

INGREDIENTS

2 tablespoons canola or grapeseed oil

1 teaspoon cumin seeds

1 red onion, chopped

1 tablespoon grated fresh ginger

1½ pounds boneless skinless chicken thighs, cut into 2-inch pieces

1 teaspoon ground turmeric

1 teaspoon cayenne pepper powder

1½ teaspoons salt

1 large (about 2 inches) cinnamon stick, broken

½ cup chopped tomatoes

1 cup packed minced kale*

1 cup packed minced spinach*

2 tablespoons fresh lime juice

Chopped cilantro to garnish

*I use a food processor for mincing the kale and spinach.

INSTRUCTIONS

1. Set the Instant Pot® to Sauté mode and heat the oil. Add the cumin seeds, and wait until the seeds begin to sizzle. Add the onion and ginger and sauté for about 5 minutes, until the onion softens and wilts.

2. Add the chicken, turmeric, cayenne pepper powder, salt, and cinnamon stick and mix well. Stir in the tomatoes, kale, and spinach.

3. Press Cancel to turn off the Sauté mode. Close the lid and set the Instant Pot® on Manual Pressure for 5 minutes.

4. When cooking time is complete, allow for Natural Pressure Release for 10 minutes.

5. Once the pressure is released, open the lid and stir in the lime juice. Place in a serving bowl, garnish with cilantro and serve.

Murgir Korma
Creamy Bengali Chicken with Almonds

Chicken Korma is a rich-tasting chicken curry with Mughal roots. This dish is often laden with cream and cashew and almond pastes, making its preparation a very laborious process. In order to make this dish accessible for every-day celebrations in my household, I replace the cream with my favorite plain Greek yogurt and add in some almond meal to thicken the sauce. I also prefer chicken on the bone for this dish as that allows for a deep and full-flavored broth.

SERVES	TOTAL TIME: 40 MINUTES	DIETARY
6	Prep Time: 5 minutes Sauté Time: 14 minutes Pressure Cook: 5 minutes Pressure Release: 10 minutes	

INGREDIENTS

2½ pounds skinless chicken on the bone (I strongly recommend dark meat)

½ cup plain Greek yogurt plus 2 tablespoons for garnish

1 teaspoon ground turmeric

1½ teaspoons salt

1 teaspoon cayenne pepper powder

3 tablespoons oil

2 medium onions, thinly sliced

1 teaspoon sugar

1 tablespoon grated fresh ginger

3 cloves garlic, minced

1½ teaspoons ground cumin

1½ teaspoons ground coriander

1 cup fresh tomato puree (about 4 tomatoes, pureed) or ½ cup canned tomato puree

¼ cup prepared almond meal (optional)

1½ teaspoons garam masala (page 31 or storebought)

1 tablespoon sliced almonds

2 teaspoons chopped cilantro

INSTRUCTIONS

1. Put the chicken in a bowl and rub with the ½ cup yogurt, turmeric, salt, and cayenne pepper powder and set aside.

2. Beat the remaining 2 tablespoons of yogurt in a separate bowl and set aside.

3. Set the Instant Pot® to Sauté mode and heat the oil. Add the sliced onions and cook for 6 to 8 minutes, gradually adding in the sugar to help with even browning. Remove about one-third of the browned onions and reserve for garnish.

4. To the remaining onions in the pot add the ginger and garlic and cook for 2 minutes. Stir in the seasoned chicken, cumin, coriander, tomato puree, almond meal (if using), and ¼ cup of water, and bring to a simmer.

5. Press Cancel to turn off the Sauté mode. Close the lid and set the Instant Pot® on Manual Pressure for 5 minutes.

6. When cooking time is complete, allow for Natural Pressure Release for 10 minutes.

7. Once the pressure is released, remove the lid and stir well. Stir in the garam masala and reserved golden onions. Place in a serving bowl, garnish with sliced almonds and drizzle with the beaten yogurt and cilantro. Serve with rice.

Chicken & Eggs   177

Bhuna Moorgi
Tender Chicken with Fragrant Spices

This dish is a classic, usually done in the Indian style of dum cooking, where the meat is browned low and slow and then sealed with a layer of dough and cooked in its own juices until it reaches golden burnished perfection. Preparing this masterpiece is simplified significantly in an Instant Pot®, in which sealed pressure cooking yields great results without any of the fuss.

SERVES

6

TOTAL TIME: 45 MINUTES
Prep Time: 7 minutes
Sauté Time: 20 minutes
Pressure Cook: 6 minutes
Pressure Release: 10 minutes

DIETARY

INGREDIENTS

¼ cup oil (mustard oil goes a long way in deepening the flavor)

2 large red onions, thinly sliced

1½ tablespoons grated fresh ginger

4 cloves garlic, minced

2 teaspoons ground cumin

1 tablespoon ground coriander

1 teaspoon cayenne pepper powder (more or less to taste)

1 large (abour 3 inch) cinnamon stick, broken into smaller pieces

4 or 5 whole cloves

4 or 5 green cardamom pods, bruised

3 or 4 bay leaves

½ teaspoon ground turmeric

1½ teaspoons salt, or to taste

3 pounds chicken on the bone or 2 pounds boneless skinless chicken thighs, cut into 2-inch pieces

2 teaspoons sugar

2 tablespoons plain yogurt, beaten till thick

3 green chilies (such as Serrano), minced

Optional Garnishes

Thinly sliced red onions

Sliced green chilies

INSTRUCTIONS

1. Set the Instant Pot® to low Sauté mode and heat the oil. Add the onions and cook for about 10 minutes, until they soften, gently wilt, and begin to turn golden. (Note: This step may take a little longer depending on the onions and the thickness of the cooker; the key is to get uniform golden brown onions—they should not be dark brown at this point.)

2. Stir in the ginger and garlic and cook for another minute. Add the cumin, coriander, and cayenne pepper powder and mix well. Add the cinnamon stick, cloves, and cardamom pods and mix well. Add the bay leaves, turmeric, salt, and chicken and sauté the chicken for about 5 minutes.

3. Stir in the sugar, yogurt, and 1 cup of water and mix well.

4. Press Cancel to turn off the Sauté mode. Close the lid and set the Instant Pot® on Manual Pressure for 6 minutes (4 minutes if using boneless chicken).

5. When cooking time is complete, allow for Natural Pressure Release for 10 minutes. Once the pressure is released, remove the lid and stir in the green chilies and mix well. Serve garnished with red onions and green chilies if desired.

Kozhi Chettinad
Chicken in Garlic Pepper Sauce

This is a signature recipe from the Chettiar community of southern India. The Instant Pot® version is a little more saucy than the traditional recipe. While the water can be cooked off, I think this version pairs beautifully with a nice steaming bowl of white rice to soak up all the sauce.

SERVES

6

TOTAL TIME: 30 MINUTES
Prep Time: 5 minutes
Sauté Time: 10 minutes
Pressure Cook: 4 minutes
Pressure Release: 10 minutes

DIETARY

INGREDIENTS

2 pounds boneless skinless chicken thighs, cut into 2-inch pieces

1 tablespoon minced garlic

1 tablespoon grated fresh ginger

1 teaspoon salt

1 teaspoon ground turmeric

2 to 3 tablespoons fresh lemon juice

2 teaspoons very coarsely ground black pepper

3 tablespoons grapeseed oil

1 teaspoon black mustard seeds

1 or 2 whole dried red chilies

10 curry leaves

2 or 3 green cardamom pods

1 or 2 star anise

1 cinnamon stick

1 medium red onion, chopped

2 tomatoes, chopped

2 to 3 tablespoons chopped cilantro

INSTRUCTIONS

1. In a mixing bowl toss the chicken with the garlic, ginger, salt, turmeric, lemon juice and 1 teaspoon of the black pepper and set aside.

2. Set the Instant Pot® on Sauté mode and heat the oil until the pot registers hot. Add the mustard seeds and wait until they begin to crackle. Add the dried red chilies, curry leaves, cardamom pods, star anise, cinnamon stick, and onion and sauté for 3 to 4 minutes.

3. Stir in the chicken mixture and cook for 3 to 4 minutes. Stir in the tomatoes.

4. Press Cancel to turn off the Sauté mode. Close the lid and set the Instant Pot® on Manual Pressure for 4 minutes.

5. When cooking time is complete, allow for Natural Pressure Release for 10 minutes.

6. Once the pressure is released, remove the lid and mix well. Stir in the remaining 1 teaspoon black pepper and the cilantro and serve.

Murgh Bhartha
Shredded Tandoori Spiced Chicken

This recipe is an adaptation of the shredded chicken usually found in roadside shops called dhabas *all across North India. Aside from the spicing, there is a difference in the texture when compared to Western-style pulled chicken dishes as the chicken in Chicken Bhartha is chunkier. It is usually served with lentils, flatbreads, and fresh cucumber salad. This dish, however, makes for a great Indian version of a pulled chicken sandwich.*

SERVES	TOTAL TIME: 30 MINUTES	DIETARY
6	Prep Time: 5 minutes plus 5 minutes shredding Sauté Time: 7 minutes Pressure Cook: 5 minutes Pressure Release: 5 minutes Broiler Time: 3 minutes	

INGREDIENTS

3 tablespoons oil

1 medium onion, minced

1 tablespoon minced garlic

1 tablespoon grated fresh ginger

2 pounds boneless skinless chicken thighs

1 tablespoons tandoori masala (page 34 or storebought)

1 teaspoon cayenne pepper powder

1 teaspoon salt

1 tomato, chopped

2 tablespoons fresh lime juice

1 tablespoon butter or ghee (page 27)

Garnish

2 tablespoons chopped cilantro

Thinly sliced red onions

Lime or lemon wedges

INSTRUCTIONS

1. Set the Instant Pot® to Sauté mode and heat the oil until the pot registers hot. Add the onion, garlic, and ginger and sauté for 5 minutes. Stir in the chicken, tandoori masala, cayenne pepper powder, salt, and tomato. Cook for another minute.

2. Press Cancel to turn off the Sauté mode. Close the lid and set the Instant Pot® on Manual Pressure for 5 minutes.

3. When the cooking time is complete, allow for Natural Pressure Release for 5 minutes, then use Quick Release for any residual pressure.

4. Once the pressure is released, open the lid and shred the chicken using two forks. If there is any excess liquid, set back on Sauté mode to evaporate, if desired.

5. Sprinkle with the lime juice and stir in the butter or ghee. Place on a heatproof serving dish and place under the broiler for 3 to 4 minutes.

6. Garnish with cilantro, sliced onions, and lime or lemon wedges.

Kashmiri Murgh
Kashmiri Chicken Curry

———

This simple comforting recipe pairs chicken with bay leaves and cardamom. The vivid red color is from Kashmiri red chili powder. The chicken absorbs the fragrant, tart seasonings, which add a lovely depth of flavor to this curry.

SERVES	TOTAL TIME: 30 MINUTES	DIETARY
6	Prep Time: 5 minutes Sauté Time: 8 minutes Pressure Cook: 4 minutes Pressure Release: 10 minutes	

INGREDIENTS

2 tablespoons grapeseed oil

1 medium onion, chopped

1 tablespoon grated fresh ginger

1 tablespoon minced garlic

2 pounds skinless boneless chicken thighs, cut into 2-inch pieces

½ teaspoon ground turmeric

2 teaspoons Kashmiri red chili powder

1 teaspoon cayenne pepper powder

2 black cardamom pods

3 green cardamom pods

1 large bay leaf

1 cup plain yogurt, beaten

2 tablespoons mint or cilantro to garnish

INSTRUCTIONS

1. Set the Instant Pot® to the Sauté mode and heat the oil for 1 minute. Add the onion, ginger, and garlic and sauté for about 3 minutes. Add the chicken and cook for 2 minutes. Stir in the turmeric, red chili powder, cayenne pepper powder, cardamom pods, and bay leaf, and cook for another minute. Stir in the salt and then use about 1 to 2 tablespoons of water to deglaze the bottom of the pot.

2. Press Cancel to turn off the Sauté mode, close the lid, and set the Instant Pot® on Manual Pressure for 4 minutes.

3. When cooking time is complete, allow for Natural Pressure Release for 10 minutes.

4. Once the pressure is released, open the lid and stir in the yogurt. Garnish with mint or cilantro before serving.

Keema Gajar Matar
Ground Chicken with Carrots, Beets and Peas

I add vegetables, such as carrots and even beets, to my Keema Matar. They not only increase the nutritional value of the dish, but also add a lovely layer of color. While Keema Matar is traditionally prepared with ground lamb, I prefer ground chicken and feel that the spices shine better with this lighter meat. You could also use ground turkey. The seasonings used in this dish vary from region to region and this particular version uses North Indian seasonings.

SERVES	TOTAL TIME: 15 MINUTES	DIETARY
4 to 6	Prep Time: 5 minutes Sauté Time: 6 minutes / 2 minutes Pressure Mode: 2 minutes	

INGREDIENTS

2 tablespoons oil

1 teaspoon cumin seeds

1 small onion, minced

1 tablespoon ground fresh ginger

3 cloves garlic, minced

4 green chilies, minced

1½ pounds ground chicken

1 medium carrot, chopped

1 medium beet, chopped

1 teaspoon salt, or to taste

1 medium tomato, chopped

1 cup frozen peas

1½ teaspoons garam masala
(page 31 or storebought)

2 tablespoons minced cilantro

INSTRUCTIONS

1. Set the Instant Pot® to Sauté mode and heat the oil for 1 minute. Add the cumin seeds and cook for a few seconds. Add the onion and sauté until wilted. Mix in the ginger, garlic, and green chilies. Add the chicken, carrot, beet, salt, and tomato and sauté to break up the chicken. Stir in 2 tablespoons water.

2. Press Cancel to turn off the Sauté mode. Close the lid and set the Instant Pot® on Manual Pressure for 2 minutes.

3. When cooking time is complete, do a Quick Pressure Release.

4. Once the pressure is released, open the lid and stir the mixture well. Set the Instant Pot® on Sauté mode again. Stir in the frozen peas and garam masala, and sauté for 2 minutes. Put mixture in a serving bowl, garnish with the cilantro, and serve.

Naga Murgh
Chicken with Green Chilies, Garlic and Green Onion

———

This very simple chicken dish is amazingly zesty and flavorful. The Naga cuisine of northeastern India is simple, but can be quite spicy. I often add in some vegetables to make this a nice cool weather stew that can be served over quinoa or rice.

SERVES

4 to 6

TOTAL TIME: 25 MINUTES
Prep Time: 5 minutes
Sauté Time: 6 minutes
Pressure Cook (Low): 4 minutes
Pressure Release: 10 minutes

DIETARY

INGREDIENTS

2 tablespoons grapeseed oil

4 cloves garlic, minced

10 green onions, chopped (whites and greens separated)

5 or 6 green chilies, minced

2 pounds boneless skinless chicken, cut into 2-inch pieces

2 tablespoons tamari

1 tomato, chopped

INSTRUCTIONS

1. Set the Instant Pot® to the Sauté mode and heat the oil. Add the garlic and scallion whites and sauté for about 3 to 4 minutes. Add the green chilies and chicken and mix well. Stir in the tamari and tomato.

2. Press Cancel to turn off the Sauté mode. Close the lid and set the Instant Pot® on Manual Low Pressure for 4 minutes.

3. When cooking time is complete, allow for Natural Pressure Release. for 10 minutes.

4. Once the pressure is released, remove the cover, stir in the reserved green onions, and serve.

Nandan Mutta Kari
Kerala Egg Curry

This is a gorgeous egg curry from Kerala. It does take a little time to get the onions to the right golden color, but that is at the heart of this dish. This curry pairs perfectly with flaky Kerala parottas, *layered flatbreads that can be found frozen in your Indian supermarket. It is typically a breakfast dish served with lacy coconut pancakes called* appams. *But let's be real, this is too much work just for breakfast! I think it is as great for dinner with a bowl of steamed rice.*

SERVES	TOTAL TIME: 35 MINUTES	DIETARY
4 to 6	Prep Time: 5 minutes Sauté Time: 10 minutes Pressure Cook (Low): 2 minutes Pressure Release: 10 minutes	

INGREDIENTS

4 tablespoons coconut oil

½ teaspoon mustard seeds

2 onions, thinly sliced

1 green chili, minced

1 tablespoon grated fresh ginger

6 cloves garlic, minced

1 teaspoon ground black pepper

½ teaspoon Kashmiri red chili powder

1 teaspoon ground fennel

2 tomatoes, chopped

1 teaspoon tamarind paste or 2 tablespoons fresh lime juice

1 cup coconut milk

10 to 12 curry leaves

1 teaspoon salt

6 to 8 hardboiled eggs, shelled

INSTRUCTIONS

1. Set the Instant Pot® to the Sauté mode and heat the oil. After a minute, add the mustard seeds and when they begin to crackle, add the onions and cook for about 5 minutes until the onions are pale golden in color.

2. Add the green chili, ginger, and garlic and mix well. Stir in the black pepper, Kashmiri red chili powder, ground fennel, tomatoes, and tamarind paste (or lime juice), and cook for another 2 minutes. Stir in the coconut milk, curry leaves, and salt.

3. Press Cancel to turn off the Sauté mode. Add in the eggs and stir to coat with sauce. Close the lid and set the Instant Pot® to Manual Low Pressure for 2 minutes.

4. When cooking time is complete, allow for Natural Pressure Release for 10 minutes. Open the lid and serve with rice.

---

*See page 27 for how to hardboil eggs in the Instant Pot®

Anda Rassa
Kolapuri Egg Curry

The Kolapur region of Maharastra is noted for its chilies, jaggery, and well-seasoned meat dishes. This egg curry incorporates the sweet and savory signature seasonings of this region. Served with rice, this is one of our favorite party-friendly egg dishes. The rassa dishes of this region are either red and tomato rich, such as this one, or white and light with coconut.

SERVES	TOTAL TIME: 15 MINUTES	DIETARY
4 to 6	Prep Time: 5 minutes Sauté Time: 5 minutes Pressure Cook (Low): 2 minutes	

INGREDIENTS

4 tablespoons oil

1 tablespoon grated fresh ginger

1 tablespoon minced garlic

2 medium red onions, minced

4 whole cloves

1 teaspoon peppercorns, slightly crushed

½ cup fresh or canned tomato puree

½ teaspoon ground turmeric

½ teaspoon cayenne pepper powder

1½ teaspoons Kashmiri red chili powder

1 teaspoon salt

1 tablespoon dried or fresh coconut

1 tablespoon poppy seeds

6 hardboiled eggs*, shelled

2 tablespoons chopped cilantro

---

*See page 27 for how to hardboil eggs in the Instant Pot®

INSTRUCTIONS

1. Set the Instant Pot® to Sauté mode and heat the oil. When oil is hot, add the ginger, garlic, and onions and sauté until onions are soft and wilted. Stir in the cloves, peppercorns, tomato puree, turmeric, and cayenne pepper powder. Stir in the Kashmiri red chili powder, salt, and ½ cup of water and bring to a simmer.

2. Grind the coconut and poppy seeds in a spice mill or coffee grinder and stir into the tomato mixture. Use an immersion blender to blend mixture until smooth. Add the eggs and stir to coat with sauce.

3. Press Cancel to turn off the Sauté mode. Close the lid, and set the Instant Pot® to Manual Low Pressure for 2 minutes.

4. When cooking time is complete, do a Quick Pressure Release. Once the pressure is released, open the lid and place eggs with sauce in a serving dish. Garnish with the cilantro, and serve with flatbreads or rice.

Dimer Jalfrezi
Eggs with Onions, Tomatoes and Bell Peppers

Jalfrezi is a light, flavorful stir-fry of Anglo-Indian origin. It was a recipe developed during colonial times as a way to use up leftover roasts and meats. I have adapted the same concept using eggs in the Instant Pot®. This quick recipe is a family favorite and something that I often cobble together, especially during summer months when my garden is brimming with peppers and tomatoes.

SERVES

4 to 6

TOTAL TIME: 15 MINUTES
Prep Time: 5 minutes
Sauté Time: 6 minutes
Pressure Cook (Low): 1 minute

DIETARY

INGREDIENTS

1 tablespoon grapeseed oil

1 teaspoon cumin seeds

4 cloves garlic, minced

½ red onion, minced plus
 1½ red onions, quartered and
 layers separated

1 green bell pepper, cut into
 wedges

1 red bell pepper, cut into
 wedges

1 tomato, quartered

½ teaspoon ground turmeric

½ teaspoon cayenne pepper
 powder

2 to 3 tablespoons plain yogurt

1 teaspoon salt

6 hardboiled eggs*, shelled

1 tablespoon chopped cilantro
 for garnish

———————

*See page 27 for how to hardboil eggs in the Instant Pot®

INSTRUCTIONS

1. Set the Instant Pot® to Sauté mode and heat the oil. Add the cumin seeds and after a few seconds, add the garlic and minced onion and cook for 3 to 4 minutes. Stir in the quartered onions, green bell pepper, red bell pepper, tomato, turmeric, cayenne pepper powder, yogurt, and salt.

2. Press Cancel to turn off the Sauté mode. Add the eggs and stir to coat with sauce. Close the lid and set the Instant Pot® to Manual Low Pressure for 1 minute.

3. When cooking time is complete, do a Quick Pressure Release. Open the lid, place in serving bowl, garnish with cilantro, and enjoy!

LAMB
& PORK

The most common variety of red meat on the Indian table is goat meat, more commonly known as mutton in India. Various parts of India, however, enjoy pork and beef as well. I have used lamb as a substitute for mutton in this book, as this is more readily available in our local grocery stores. In this chapter, I offer a selection of a few classic recipes which are in line with the prominence of red meat on the Indian table. Due to the complexity of cooking it, meat is more of a celebratory food in India, served for festive occasions. In Indian cooking, the preference is to use meat on the bone with most fat trimmed off. In cooler parts of the country such as the Kashmiri highlands, however, the fat is often incorporated in the cooking as an additional fortification against the cold.

Meat is usually cooked until fork tender—to a fall-off-the-bone consistency that's achieved fairly easily in the Instant Pot®. It is important to take the time to sear and cook the spices with the meat. This process, called *"bhunao,"* is extremely important in deepening the flavor of the dish. Though the searing process can take a while, in the following recipes I simplified it considerably to save time. With an Instant Pot®, the meat is cooking in its own juices and the moisture is sealed, so you end up with a very flavorful, tender result. Please also note that water needs to be added according to recipe instructions, so that you do not end up with a very soupy dish.

Dahi Pudina Gosht
Yogurt Mint Lamb Curry

———

This very basic lamb curry from the Punjabi winter table is made super simple and accessible with the use of two make-ahead ingredients. The mushrooms add an earthy depth of flavor and the carrots and mint round off the dish with a nice dose of fragrant sweetness.

SERVES

4 to 6

TOTAL TIME: 40 MINUTES
Prep Time: 5 minutes
Meat/Stew Mode: 20 minutes
Pressure Release: 10 minutes
Sauté/Finish Time: 5 minutes

DIETARY

INGREDIENTS

2 pounds boneless lamb, trimmed and cut into 2-inch pieces

1½ cups Everyday Masala Paste (see page 29)

1 teaspoon salt, or to taste

1 teaspoon cayenne pepper powder, or to taste

1½ cups button mushrooms, quartered

3 carrots, peeled and cut into thirds

½ cup fresh mint

¼ cup plain yogurt, beaten

1½ teaspoons garam masala (page 31 or storebought)

INSTRUCTIONS

1. Place the lamb, masala paste, salt, cayenne pepper powder, and mushrooms in the Instant Pot®. Mix well. Close the lid and set the Instant Pot® on the Meat/Stew mode for 20 minutes.

2. When cooking time is complete, allow for Natural Pressure Release for about 10 minutes, then use Quick Release for any residual pressure.

3. In the meantime, place the carrots and mint in a food processor and process until finely chopped.

4. Stir the carrot mixture and yogurt into the lamb. Set the Instant Pot® on Sauté mode. Simmer for 5 minutes.

5. Stir in the garam masala before serving.

Laal Maas
Rajasthan Red Lamb Curry

———

Laal Maas is a bold, full-flavored curry from the princely state of Rajasthan. I confess that in order to achieve the rich red color and authentic heat of this dish, I would need to increase the amount of red chilies. But I believe the amounts in my variation allow for a decent amount of spice without making the dish overwhelmingly hot. The Instant Pot® allowed me to lighten this dish from the traditional because it seals the flavors—the traditional recipe does this with lots of clarified butter or ghee including a good dollop of ghee with garlic at the end. I skip the finishing ghee and the dish still tastes delicious.

SERVES	TOTAL TIME: 55 MINUTES (plus 6 hours marinating)	DIETARY
4 to 6	Prep Time: 5 minutes plus 6 hours marinating Sauté Time: 10 minutes Meat/Stew Mode: 25 minutes Pressure Release: 10 minutes Resting Time: 2 minutes	

INGREDIENTS

2 pounds leg of lamb on the bone, trimmed and cut into 2-inch pieces

1½ teaspoons salt

2 tablespoons oil

1 cup chopped red onion

1 or 2 (2-inch) cinnamon sticks

2 black cardamom pods

1 cup plain lowfat Greek yogurt

2 tablespoons minced garlic

Chopped cilantro to garnish

For marinade:

2-inch piece ginger, peeled

6 cloves garlic, peeled

1 tablespoon ground cumin

1 tablespoon ground coriander

5 dried red chilies, ground (about 1 tablespoon)

1 tablespoon Kashmiri red chili powder or paprika

INSTRUCTIONS

Marinate the lamb:

1. Prepare the marinade: puree the ginger and garlic into a paste and mix in the cumin, coriander, ground red chilies, and Kashmiri red chili powder (or paprika). Rub the marinade onto the lamb. Sprinkle the salt over the lamb and stir in. Set the lamb aside to marinate in the refrigerator for 6 hours or overnight.

Prepare curry:

2. Set the Instant Pot® to Sauté mode and heat the oil. Add the onion and cook, stirring frequently, until it begins to sweat and turn golden, about 5 minutes. Stir in the cinnamon sticks, cardamom pods, and marinated lamb and sauté for about 4 minutes. Add the yogurt and mix well.

3. Press Cancel to turn off the Sauté mode. Close the lid and set the Instant Pot® on the Meat/Stew mode for 25 minutes.

4. When cooking time is complete, allow for Natural Pressure Release for about 10 minutes, then use Quick Release for any residual pressure.

5. Once the pressure is released, remove the lid and stir in the minced garlic. Cover and let it rest for 2 minutes. Serve garnished with the chopped cilantro.

Rogan Josh
Kashmiri Fragrant Lamb Curry

Often after a busy day, this delicate, flavorful dish calls my name. It is essential to have Kashmiri red chili powder on hand, as this bright, fragrant spice is what colors this dish without adding an inordinate amount of heat. (If you cannot find Kashmiri red chili powder, ancho chili powder is a better substitute than paprika for this particular dish.) Traditionally this recipe is made with rich, fatty cuts of goat meat, but since lamb is more flavorful than goat meat, trimming the fat off gives this dish just the right amount of richness. The list of ingredients might seem a little daunting, but most are just easily added to the curry.

SERVES	TOTAL TIME: 45 MINUTES	DIETARY
4 to 6	Prep Time: 5 minutes Sauté Time: 10 minutes Meat/Stew Mode: 20 minutes Pressure Release: 10 minutes	

INGREDIENTS

2 tablespoons oil

1 large red onion, chopped (about 1¼ cups)

1 tablespoon minced fresh ginger

1 tablespoon minced garlic

1 tablespoon Kashmiri red chili powder

1 teaspoon cayenne pepper powder

1 teaspoon ground fennel

1 teaspoon ground nutmeg

4 to 6 green cardamom pods

2 whole black cardamom pods

1 large cinnamon stick

2 or 3 bay leaves

1½ teaspoons salt, or to taste

1½ pounds boneless lamb, trimmed and cubed

2 tomatoes, chopped

½ cup lowfat plain yogurt, beaten

Chopped cilantro to garnish

INSTRUCTIONS

1. Set the Instant Pot® to Sauté mode and heat the oil. After the Instant Pot® registers hot, add the onion, ginger, and garlic, and sauté for about 5 minutes, until the onions turn translucent and wilt considerably.

2. Add the Kashmiri red chili powder, cayenne pepper powder, fennel, nutmeg, cardamom pods, cinnamon stick, and bay leaves, and stir lightly. Stir in the salt and lamb and cook for a few minutes until the lamb changes color slightly. Add the tomatoes, yogurt, and ½ cup of water and mix well.

3. Press Cancel to turn off the Sauté mode, close the lid, and set the Instant Pot® on the Meat/Stew mode for 20 minutes.

4. When cooking time is complete, allow for Natural Pressure Release for 10 minutes, then use Quick Release for any residual pressure.

5. Once the pressure is released, open the lid, remove the stew from the pot, and garnish with cilantro. Serve with steamed rice for a satisfying meal.

Gosht Dhansak
Lamb with Lentils and Vegetables

Dhansak is a signature dish from the Parsee community in western India. This traditional Sunday supper is usually complemented by Parsee Brown Rice (page 65) and a light, fresh salad. The characteristic flavors of this complex dish are a well-seasoned composition with sweet and tart notes. The list of spices might seem a little daunting, and if you want to make it easier, you can certainly replace the fresh spice blend with storebought dhansak masala. Good homemade Dhansak can be the ultimate comforting soul food, perfect for a Sunday family meal. My recipe is adapted and simplified from one I found in Times of India.

SERVES

4 to 6

TOTAL TIME: 70 MINUTES
Prep Time: 15 minutes
Sauté Time: 12 minutes
Pressure Cook: 25 minutes
Pressure Release: 15 minutes

DIETARY

INGREDIENTS

For spice blend:

1 teaspoon cardamom seeds

10 whole cloves

1 large cinnamon stick

1 teaspoon ground nutmeg

2 or 3 blades mace

1 teaspoon fennel seeds

2 teaspoons cumin seeds

2 teaspoons coriander seeds

INSTRUCTIONS

Make spice blend:

1. Place all the ingredients for the spice blend in a spice mill or coffee grinder and grind until smooth. Set aside.

For Dhansak:

¼ cup oil

1 large onion, minced

1 tablespoon minced garlic

1 tablespoon grated fresh ginger

1 pound lamb on the bone (leg and rib pieces), trimmed and cut into 2-inch pieces

½ cup chopped mint leaves or 1 teaspoon dried mint

1 tablespoon minced green chilies (about 3)

1 teaspoon Kashmiri red chili powder

2 tablespoons tamarind paste or 3 tablespoons fresh lime juice

2 teaspoons salt, or to taste

2 tomatoes, chopped

¼ cup split pigeon peas (toor dal)

¼ cup red split lentils (masoor dal)

¼ cup split Bengal gram lentils (chana dal)

2 cups cubed pumpkin or butternut squash

1 small eggplant, cubed

1 tablespoon dried fenugreek leaves (kasuri methi)

1 tablespoon brown sugar

Garnishes

2 tablespoons chopped cilantro

1 tablespoon pomegranate seeds (optional)

Prepare Dhansak:

2. Set the Instant Pot® to Sauté mode and heat the oil. Add the onions and cook for about 5 minutes. Add the garlic, ginger, and lamb and cook until the meat is no longer pink.

3. Add the prepared Spice Blend and the mint, green chilies, Kashmiri chili powder, tamarind paste or lime juice, salt, and tomatoes. Cook for another minute. Add all the lentils/dals and the pumpkin (or squash), eggplant, fenugreek leaves, and brown sugar and give it a good stir.

4. Press Cancel to turn off the Sauté mode. Stir in about 5 cups water and close the lid. Set the Instant Pot® to Manual Pressure for 25 minutes.

5. When cooking time is complete, allow for Natural Pressure Release for about 15 minutes.

6. Once the pressure is released, remove the lid and remove the lamb pieces from the sauce. Mix the lentil mixture well and either puree with an immersion blender or beat well with a whisk.

7. Return the lamb to the sauce and serve garnished with the cilantro and pomegranate seeds (if using).

> *Note:*
> The vegetarian version of this dish is also great and I often make it on weeknights with seasonal vegetables on hand.

Mashor Jhol
Oriya Lamb Curry with Potatoes

Potatoes hold center stage alongside the lamb in this nuanced curry from Odhisha. The gravy is relatively thin and subtly spiced, though the fragrance of ginger is quite distinct. It makes for an excellent party dish and can be made ahead as it tastes even better the next day. This curry is best served with steamed rice or chapatis.

SERVES

4 to 6

TOTAL TIME: 55 MINUTES
Prep Time: 10 minutes
Sauté Time: 12 minutes
Pressure Cook: 25 minutes
Pressure Release: 5 minutes

DIETARY

INGREDIENTS

3 tablespoons mustard oil

1 medium onion, thinly sliced

2 tablespoons grated fresh ginger

1 or 2 bay leaves

1 (3-inch) cinnamon stick

4 green cardamom pods

3 or 4 whole cloves

1½ pounds boneless lamb, trimmed of all visible fat

½ teaspoon ground turmeric

1 teaspoon cayenne pepper powder

½ cup plain yogurt

1 teaspoon salt

1 teaspoon sugar

4 to 6 baby potatoes, peeled

1 tablespoon chopped cilantro to garnish

> *Note:*
> You can add the whole spices in a tea ball, so that they can be removed easily later.

INSTRUCTIONS

1. Set the Instant Pot® to Sauté mode and heat the mustard oil for 1 minute. Add the onion and ginger and cook for 4 minutes. Add the bay leaves, cinnamon stick, cardamom pods, cloves, lamb, turmeric, and cayenne pepper powder, and sear the lamb for 4 to 5 minutes.

2. Stir in the yogurt, salt, and sugar and cook for another 2 minutes. Stir in ½ cup of water and the potatoes.

3. Press Cancel to turn off the Sauté mode. Close the lid and set the Instant Pot® on Manual Pressure for 25 minutes.

4. When the cooking time is complete, allow for Natural Pressure Release for 5 minutes and then use Quick Release for any residual pressure. Once the pressure is released, open the pot and serve the lamb curry garnished with cilantro.

Masala Chaamp
Well-Seasoned Braised Lamb Chops

This recipe for lamb chops is from Hyderabad in South India. The original recipe includes multiples steps, but I managed to cut them down by adding in the process of marinating. This dish requires a little planning, but practically no hands-on involvement or time.

SERVES

4 to 6

TOTAL TIME: 35 MINUTES (plus 6 hours marinating)
Prep Time: 10 minutes plus 6 hours
Sauté Time: 10 minutes
Pressure Cook: 8 minutes
Pressure Release: 5 minutes

DIETARY

INGREDIENTS

2 pounds lamb rib chops

2 tablespoons coconut oil

1 large onion, thinly sliced

1 teaspoon Kashmiri red chili powder

1 teaspoon cayenne pepper powder

10 curry leaves

2 tablespoons plain yogurt

2 tablespoons fresh lime juice

1 tablespoon chopped cilantro

For marinade:

1½ teaspoons fennel seeds

1 teaspoon black peppercorns

1 cinnamon stick

10 green cardamom pods

1 teaspoon whole cloves

1-inch piece ginger, peeled

1 teaspoon salt

INSTRUCTIONS

Marinate lamb chops:

1. Place the fennel seeds, black peppercorns, cinnamon stick, cardamom pods, cloves, ginger, and salt in a blender with 2 tablespoons water. Pulse several times to break down the ingredients and then grind to a smooth puree. (Alternately, grind the dry spices to a powder in a spice mill and then blend with the ginger and salt.) In a bowl toss the lamb chops with the marinade to coat and marinate in the refrigerator for at least 6 hours.

Braise lamb chops:

2. Set the Instant Pot® to Sauté mode and heat the coconut oil. After a minute add the onion and cook for 5 minutes. Stir in the lamb chops with the marinade and cook for 3 to 4 minutes. Stir in the Kashmiri red chili powder, cayenne pepper powder, curry leaves, and yogurt.

3. Press Cancel to turn off the Sauté mode. Close the lid and set the Instant Pot® on Manual Pressure for 8 minutes.

4. When cooking time is complete, allow for Natural Pressure Release for about 5 minutes and then use Quick Release for any residual pressure.

5. Once the pressure is released, open the lid and transfer lamb chops to a serving platter and sprinkle with lime juice and garnish with cilantro before serving.

Pork Vindaloo
Pork Ribs in Spicy Garlic Chili Sauce

Goan cuisine features a fair amount of pork, with Pork Vindaloo being the signature offering. For this recipe, I was inspired by a stove-top version by noted Goan chef Floyd Cardoz, and decided to make it with ribs instead. I simplified the list of ingredients and the Instant Pot® cut down the cooking time considerably. If you are a fan of meat and spices, this recipe is for you.

SERVES	TOTAL TIME: 60 MINUTES	DIETARY
4 to 6	Prep Time: 10 minutes Sauté Time: 10 minutes Meat/Stew Mode: 25 minutes Pressure Release: 10 minutes	

INGREDIENTS

1 tablespoon salt

1½ pounds baby back ribs

2 whole dried red chilies

1 tablespoon cumin seeds

2 whole cloves

1 (2-inch) cinnamon stick

2 tablespoons Kashmiri red chili powder

1 teaspoon ground turmeric

3 tablespoons oil

1 cup minced red onion

3 tablespoons minced garlic

1 tablespoon minced ginger

¼ cup red wine vinegar

¾ cup low-sodium chicken or vegetable broth

3 tablespoons brown sugar

Chopped green onions for garnish

Crushed red pepper for garnish

INSTRUCTIONS

1. Sprinkle salt over the ribs. If needed cut the ribs into smaller pieces to fit in the Instant Pot®. Set aside while continuing with the rest of the prepping.

2. Place the dried chilies, cumin seeds, cloves, cinnamon stick, Kashmiri red chili powder, and turmeric in a spice mill or coffee grinder and grind to a powder.

3. Set the Instant Pot® to Sauté mode, and heat the oil for about 1 minute. Add the red onion, garlic, and ginger and sauté for about 2 minutes. Stir in the ground spice mixture and vinegar. Add the ribs and cook, stirring, until the ribs are coated and the mixture is a rich reddish-brown color, about 3 minutes. Add the chicken or vegetable broth and brown sugar and stir well. Bring the mixture to a simmer.

4. Press Cancel to turn off the Sauté mode. Close the lid and set the Instant Pot® on the Meat/Stew mode for 25 minutes.

5. When cooking time is complete, allow for Natural Pressure Release for 10 minutes, then use Quick Release for any residual pressure.

6. Once the pressure is released, open the lid and set the Instant Pot® to Sauté mode and simmer to thicken the liquid. Drain off any excess fat.

7. Garnish with the green onions and crushed red pepper and serve with steamed rice or crusty bread.

DESSERTS
& DRINKS

Indian desserts are notoriously laborious and time-consuming but often well worth the effort. I personally am of the belief that a good Indian meal is incomplete without some masala chai and a touch of sweetness. To this end, this chapter offers you some of the essential Indian dessert recipes. Some of the features of the Instant Pot®, such as the consistent high heat and the fermentation and steaming features work very well for several of the Indian desserts. Indian puddings such as a halwa and kheer all can be cooked quite easily in the Instant Pot®. In fact, many Indian households have been doing these successfully in the pressure cooker for

Mango Lassi (page 228)

years. In selecting the recipes for this chapter, however, my intent was to offer you an assortment of techniques that can be adapted or diversified for other desserts.

When you do not have time to rustle up any of these desserts, find some fresh fruit and whip yourself a fresh lassi. These yogurt smoothies are delicious, traditional, and very good for you.

Amritsari Phirni
Rice and Almond Pudding with Cardamom

An Indian cookbook would be incomplete without at least one recipe for rice pudding. The more common variety is called kheer *or* payesam. *Phirni is an adaptation made with broken rice which cooks much quicker. It is popular in the Punjabi city of Amritsar and is often served for festive occasions. I have seen modern variations using rice flour, but please do not use that as it does not have the slight grainy texture that is essential for this recipe. I do not use the pressure cooker for this recipe as it cooks pretty quickly and the ground rice can clump if not stirred frequently. This dessert can be made with almond milk for a vegan variation.*

SERVES	TOTAL TIME: 1 HOUR AND 15 MINUTES	DIETARY
4 to 6	Prep Time: 5 minutes Sauté Time: 10 minutes Chill Time: 1 hour	

INGREDIENTS

4 tablespoons basmati rice

¼ teaspoon cardamom seeds

2 quarts (8 cups) whole milk or almond milk

½ teaspoon saffron strands

¾ cup sugar

½ cup almond meal

Chopped almonds and pistachios to garnish

INSTRUCTIONS

1. Place the basmati rice and cardamom seeds in a spice mill or coffee grinder and grind for 1 minute—you want a powder with just a hint of texture.

2. Place the milk in the Instant Pot and set to Sauté mode. Once it reaches a simmer, stir in the rice mixture. Simmer the mixture, stirring occasionally, for about 7 minutes. When the mixture is thickened and the rice is soft, stir in the saffron strands, sugar, and almond meal. Cook for another 3 to 4 minutes.

3. Press Cancel to turn off the Sauté mode. Pour the pudding into a serving bowl and chill for at least an hour, or longer if time permits.

4. Serve the chilled pudding garnished with almonds and pistachios.

Shakarkandi Halwa
Cardamom and Sweet Potato Pudding

———

A beautiful fall-to-winter dessert that will add the right amount of color and indulgence to your table, this captures the natural sweetness of the sweet potato and accentuates it with brown sugar and raisins. A halwa is the Indian equivalent of a pudding, and this recipe is from the northern state of Uttar Pradesh.

SERVES	TOTAL TIME: 20 MINUTES	DIETARY
8 to 10	Prep Time: 3 minutes Pressure Cook: 7 minutes Sauté Time: 10 minutes	

INGREDIENTS

6 medium sweet potatoes (about 1½ pounds; I use the orange North Carolina variety)

1 cup whole milk (or half and half if you are feeling indulgent)

½ cup brown sugar

4 green cardamom pods, gently bruised

½ cup green or golden raisins

¼ cup ghee (page 27)

¼ cup sliced or slivered almonds

1 teaspoon crushed dried rose petals (optional)

INSTRUCTIONS

1. Peel and halve the sweet potatoes and place in the Instant Pot® with the milk, brown sugar, and cardamom pods. Close the lid, and set the Instant Pot® on Manual Pressure for 7 minutes.

2. When the cooking time is complete, use Quick Pressure Release. Once the pressure is released, open the lid, remove the whole cardamom pods, then mash the sweet potatoes with the milk. Stir in the raisins.

3. Set the Instant Pot® on the Sauté mode and cook for about 5 to 6 minutes, stirring frequently. At this point, the mixture should form a smooth, fairly thick mass and move with the direction of the spoon. Stir in the ghee and cook for another 4 minutes.

4. Place sweet potato mixture in a serving bowl and garnish with slivered almonds and the rose petals, if using. Serve the halwa warm.

Roshogolla
Cheese Balls in Cardamom Syrup

A fresh-tasting dessert that is an heirloom recipe from eastern India, Roshogolla is prized enough to actually have created an agreement between the states of Odhisha and West Bengal over its origin. Currently, West Bengal has a "geographical indication" or GI status over this delicate confectionary. Roshogolla is not difficult to prepare, however the devil is in the details. The whey needs to be completely drained out to result in spongy, soft cheese balls. It is also important to let the pressure release naturally and then rest for 10 more minutes before opening the lid to allow for a spongy well-cooked consistency.

SERVES	TOTAL TIME: 3 HOURS & 15 MINUTES	DIETARY
4 to 6	Prep Time: 7 minutes Drain Time: 2 hours Pressure Cook (Low): 5 minutes Pressure Release and Rest Time: 1 hour	

INGREDIENTS

½ gallon whole milk

2 to 4 tablespoons lime juice

2 or 3 green cardamom pods

2 cups sugar

1 tablespoon fine semolina or all-purpose flour

A few slivered almonds to garnish (optional)

INSTRUCTIONS

1. Heat the milk until it comes to a rolling boil in a large pot on the stovetop. Turn off the heat. While the milk is still very hot, stir in the lime juice about 1 tablespoon at a time until the cheese curds separate from the whey. Line a colander with cheesecloth and pour the milk mixture in. Allow to drain for about 2 hours— the cheese is ready when there is no obvious water dripping, but it is not too dry.

2. In the meantime, set the Instant Pot® to Sauté mode and add the cardamom pods, sugar, and ½ cup of water and bring to a boil. Let it boil for 25 to 30 minutes until a light syrup is formed. Press Cancel to turn off Instant Pot®.

3. Place the drained fresh cheese and the semolina or all-purpose flour in a food processor and blend for about 1 minute. Gather the cheese into a ball and then break off pieces and form small walnut-sized balls. Cover the balls with a moist, thin cloth and let them rest for about 3 minutes.

4. Gently lower the cheese balls into the sugar syrup in the Instant Pot® and carefully toss to coat. Close the lid and set the Instant Pot® on Manual Low Pressure for 5 minutes.

5. When the cooking time is complete, turn the pot off and leave undisturbed for 1 hour before opening.

6. Open the lid and remove the cheese balls from the pot and place in a bowl with half the poaching syrup. Serve hot or chilled garnished with the almonds.

Rasmalai
Sweet Cheese Disks in Cream Sauce

Rasmalai is a popular dessert all across India, but has its origins in northern India. It is similar in some ways to Roshogolla (page 216), but is garnished with nuts and raisins and has the added decadence of a creamy sauce. I like to use a mixture of golden and green raisins if possible, to give the dish a nice pop of color.

SERVES

4 to 6

TOTAL TIME: 4 HOURS AND 15 MINUTES
Prep Time: 10 minutes
Drain Time: 2 hours
Pressure Cook (Low): 5 minutes
Pressure Release and Rest Time: 1 hour
Chill Time: 1 hour

DIETARY

INGREDIENTS

1 gallon whole milk (16 cups)

2 to 4 tablespoons fresh lime juice

2 or 3 green cardamom pods

3 cups sugar

1 tablespoon fine semolina or all-purpose flour

Assorted raisins

Chopped almonds to garnish

INSTRUCTIONS

1. Heat half a gallon (8 cups) of the milk until it comes to a rolling boil in a large pot on the stovetop. Turn off the heat. While the milk is still very hot, stir in the lime juice about 1 tablespoon at a time until the cheese curds separate from the whey. Line a colander with cheesecloth and pour the milk mixture in. Allow to drain for about 2 hours—the cheese is ready when there is no obvious water dripping, but it is not too dry.

2. In the meantime, set the Instant Pot® to Sauté mode and add the cardamom pods, sugar, and 1½ cups of water and bring to a boil. Let it boil for 25 to 30 minutes until a light syrup is formed. Press Cancel to turn off Instant Pot®.

3. Place the drained fresh cheese and the semolina or all-purpose flour in a food processor and blend for about 1 minute. Gather the cheese into a ball and then break off pieces and form into small oval disks. Cover the cheese disks with a moist, thin cloth and let them rest for about 3 minutes.

4. Gently lower the cheese disks into the sugar syrup in the Instant Pot® and carefully toss to coat. Close the lid and set the Instant Pot® on Manual Low Pressure for 5 minutes. When the cooking time is complete, turn the pot off and leave undisturbed for 1 hour before opening.

5. Meanwhile, in a separate saucepan, boil the remaining ½ gallon of milk (8 cups) until reduced by half.

6. After the cheese disks have rested for 1 hour, open the Instant Pot® and place the disk and ½ cup to 1 cup of the sugar syrup (depending on desired sweetness) in the pan with the reduced milk and stir gently to combine. Chill for at least 1 hour.

7. Garnish the chilled cheese with the raisins and nuts before serving.

Desserts & Drinks

Mishti Doi

Sweetened Yogurt

Mishti Doi is a signature dish from West Bengal. It is made with thickened milk, flavored with a hint of caramelized sugar, and then set like regular yogurt. The Instant Pot® assures a well-set yogurt that is done in a fuss-free manner. While you can certainly use the method described on page 25 to make your own evaporated milk, this is one of those desserts where using the canned evaporated milk actually does not impact the taste.

SERVES	TOTAL TIME: 8 HOURS & 15 MINUTES	DIETARY
4 to 6	Prep Time: 15 minutes Yogurt Setting: 8 hours	

INGREDIENTS

⅓ cup plus 2 tablespoons sugar (use more if you prefer a sweeter dessert)

2 cups evaporated milk (homemade, page 25, or canned)

¼ cup plain Greek yogurt or homemade yogurt starter

INSTRUCTIONS

1. Place the 2 tablespoons sugar and 1 tablespoons of water in a large pan and cook on medium-low heat until it bubbles and turns into a golden caramel. Quickly add the evaporated milk and bring the milk to a boil. Remove from heat and stir in the remaining ⅓ cup sugar and then allow the milk to cool down to 60 degrees.

2. Once the milk is cooled to 60 degrees, stir in the yogurt starter. Pour into a non-reactive bowl such as a steel bowl. Place the bowl in the Instant Pot®. Close the lid and set the Instant Pot® on Yogurt mode (8 hours).

3. When cooking time is complete, open the lid and chill the yogurt before serving.

Lagan Nu Custard
Indian Baked Custard

———

For my daughter's fifteenth birthday, we needed a unique dessert. Like a good desi mom, I found something that would work on a weeknight evening and still be special. My find was this Parsee custard, whose name translates as "wedding custard" since it is served at weddings or engagements. "Lagan" means joining or coming together. Parsee cuisine brings together an interesting confluence of culinary influences as is seen in the use of nutmeg, cardamom, and vanilla in this dessert.

SERVES	TOTAL TIME: 5 HOURS AND 40 MINUTES	DIETARY
4 to 6	Prep Time: 10 minutes Steam Time: 15 minutes Pressure Release: 15 minutes Chilling Time: 5 hours	

INGREDIENTS

1½ cups whole milk

2 eggs

½ cup sugar

1 teaspoon vanilla extract

¼ teaspoon ground nutmeg

¼ teaspoon ground cardamom

1 tablespoon ghee (page 27)

2 tablespoons chopped cashews

2 tablespoons chopped pistachios

2 tablespoons pinenuts

1 tablespoon raisins

INSTRUCTIONS

1. Grease a 6-inch round casserole or heatproof dish with oil and set aside.

2. In a mixing bowl, beat together the milk, eggs, sugar, vanilla, nutmeg, and cardamom. Pour the mixture into the greased casserole dish and cover with aluminum foil.

3. Place a trivet in the Instant Pot®. Add 1½ cups water. Place the casserole on the trivet. Close the lid, and set the Instant Pot® to Steam mode for 15 minutes.

4. When the cooking time is complete, allow for Natural Pressure Release for about 15 minutes.

5. Once the pressure is released, open the lid and remove the casserole dish. Chill custard in refrigerator for 4 to 5 hours.

6. When ready to serve, heat the ghee in a small pan and add the cashews, pistachios, pine nuts, and raisins and sauté until the nuts are lightly toasted. Pour over the chilled custard before serving.

Kesar Bhapa Sandesh
Steamed Saffron Cheesecake

After spending weeks trying to come up with an adapted recipe for cheesecake I remembered this steamed recipe from the Bengali table. A sandesh is made from fresh paneer/chenna and can be cooked on the stovetop or by gently steaming it. This is usually a carefully coordinated process, but is naturally very easy when done in the Instant Pot®. Other than planning ahead to make and drain the paneer/chenna this recipe practically cooks itself.

SERVES	TOTAL TIME: 2 TO 4 HOURS	DIETARY
6 to 8	Prep Time: 5 minutes plus 45 minutes to drain paneer Steam Time (Low): 15 minutes Pressure Release: 10 minutes Chilling Time: 1 to 4 hours	

INGREDIENTS

1 recipe paneer/chenna made with ½ gallon milk (page 26), drained for at least 45 minutes

½ cup sugar

1½ tablespoons fine semolina

½ teaspoon freshly ground cardamom

½ teaspoon saffron strands

Chopped pistachios to garnish (optional)

INSTRUCTIONS

1. Place the drained paneer/chenna in a food processor, add the sugar and semolina and process for about 1 minute until well mixed—the mixture should gather into a ball. Add the ground cardamom and saffron and process to combine.

2. Grease a 6-inch round baking dish, then put in the cheese mixture and spread evenly. Cover well with foil. Place a trivet in the Instant Pot® and add water. Place the pan with the cheese mixture on the trivet and close lid. Set the Instant Pot® on Low Steam mode for 15 minutes.

3. When cooking time is complete, allow for Natural Pressure Release for about 10 minutes and then use Quick Release for any residual pressure.

4. Place the cheesecake in the refrigerator and chill for 1 to 4 hours. When ready to serve, remove the cheesecake from pan, cut into wedges, and serve garnished with pistachios.

Khubani Ka Meetha
Poached Apricots with Whipped Cream

This easy and luscious offering is from the southern city of Hyderabad. It is really as simple as it sounds. Fresh apricots are poached in a cardamom-laced syrup and served with whipped cream. Dried apricots can also be used for this recipe; they just need to be stewed a little longer. The desired texture of the fruit is somewhere between a poached fruit and a compote. I like to keep this closer to poached fruit, though traditionally it is stewed and cooked down to compote. The operative word of "between" leaves so much to interpretation!

SERVES	TOTAL TIME: 2 HOURS AND 15 MINUTES	DIETARY
4 to 6	Prep Time: 10 minutes Pressure Cook: 1 to 3 minutes Chilling Time: 2 hours	

INGREDIENTS

½ cup sugar

15 fresh apricots or 20 dried apricots

6 to 8 green cardamom pods

1 cup heavy cream, whipped

1 teaspoon rosewater

Sliced almonds and/or pistachios

INSTRUCTIONS

1. Set the Instant Pot® to Sauté mode. Add the sugar and 1½ cups of water and bring to a simmer. While this is simmering, cut the fresh apricots in half and remove the center stones.

2. Once the sugar water is simmering, press Cancel to turn off the Sauté mode. Stir in the cardamom pods and apricots. Close the lid and set the Instant Pot® on Manual Pressure for 1 minute if using fresh apricots or 3 minutes if using dried apricots.

3. When the cooking time is complete, do a Quick Pressure Release. Open the lid, and let the apricots cool slightly. Place in a serving bowl and chill for at least 2 hours.

4. Serve the apricots with some whipped cream garnished with rosewater and almonds and/or pistachios.

Sevai
Vermicelli and Date Pudding

This vermicelli pudding, almost as classic as rice pudding, is enjoyed in different forms all over India. Also known as Sheer Korma, it is a signature dessert during the Muslim festival of Eid. Dates are usually a mandatory addition to this dessert. It is not complex, but you do need to reduce the milk, which takes some time although not necessarily much attention.

SERVES	TOTAL TIME: 50 MINUTES	DIETARY
6	Prep Time: 5 minutes Sauté Time: 45 minutes	

INGREDIENTS

1 gallon whole milk (16 cups)

5 green cardamom pods

1 cup roasted wheat vermicelli, broken into pieces

¾ cup sugar

¾ cup chopped dates

1 teaspoon rosewater

¼ cup chopped pistachios

¼ cup chopped almonds

INSTRUCTIONS

1. Set the Instant Pot® to Sauté mode. Add the milk and cardamom pods and bring to a simmer. Stirring occasionally, simmer the milk until it is reduced to two-thirds of its original volume (10 cups), about 40 minutes.

2. Add the wheat vermicelli and sugar and stir well. Add the dates and simmer for 3 to 4 minutes. Stir in the rosewater.

3. Serve warm or cold, garnished with the pistachios and almonds..

Meetha Lassi
Sweet Yogurt Drink

SERVES 4

INGREDIENTS

3 cups plain yogurt

½ cup sugar

INSTRUCTIONS

Place the yogurt, sugar, and 1½ cups of water in a blender and blend until smooth. Serve in glasses with ice if desired.

SWEET LASSI VARIATIONS

Mango Lassi: Replace ½ cup yogurt with 1 cup fresh or frozen mango pieces.

Strawberry Lassi: Replace ½ cup yogurt with 1 cup chopped strawberries and a handful of fresh mint leaves.

Kesar Pista Lassi: Add ¼ cup chopped pistachios and ¼ teaspoon saffron strands

Banana Lassi: Replace ½ cup yogurt with 2 bananas and ¼ teaspoon cinnamon. (Please check sweetness here, because some ripe bananas can be very sweet.)

Namkeen Lassi
Savory Yogurt Drink

SERVES 4

INGREDIENTS

3 cups plain yogurt

¾ teaspoon salt

¼ teaspoon black pepper

INSTRUCTIONS

Place the yogurt, salt, pepper and 1½ cups of water in a blender and blend until smooth. Serve in glasses with ice if desired.

SAVORY LASSI VARIATIONS

Cumin and Cilantro: Add 1 teaspoon toasted cumin seeds and ¼ cup chopped cilantro

South Indian: Heat 1 teaspoon of oil and add ½ teaspoon mustard seeds and wait until the seeds pop. Add the toasted mustard seeds, 10 curry leaves, and a pinch of asafoetida when blending the lassi.

Masala Chai
Indian Spiced Tea

Spiced tea holds a very special place on the Indian table. There are many spice blends and variations for this energizing fragrant brew, but this is my version adapted for the Instant Pot®. The preferred tea for making masala chai is a strong black tea such as Assam or Nilgiri. Whole spices are great as they can be strained out, or you can use a tea ball for both the tea and the spices.

SERVES	TOTAL TIME: 15 MINUTES	DIETARY
4 to 6	Prep Time: 2 minutes Pressure Cook: 4 minutes Pressure Release: 5 minutes	

INGREDIENTS

2 tablespoons loose black tea leaves

2 cups whole or 2% milk

1 large (about 3 inches) cinnamon stick

1 teaspoon black peppercorns

2 star anise

2 green cardamom pods

1-inch piece fresh ginger, peeled and thinly sliced

Sugar to taste

INSTRUCTIONS

1. Put the tea, milk, cinnamon stick, peppercorns, star anise, cardamom pods, ginger, and 2 cups of water in the Instant Pot®.

2. Close the lid and set the Instant Pot® on Manual Pressure for 4 minutes.

3. When cooking time is complete, allow for Natural Pressure Release for 5 minutes, then use Quick Release for any residual pressure. Open the lid and strain the tea. Sweeten to taste and serve.

CHUTNEYS
& RAITA

The final chapter in this book features condiments. As with some of the basic spice recipes in Chapter 2, some of these recipes are not made in the Instant Pot®. I wanted to include them here though since no Indian meal is complete without condiments.

Condiments accent all kinds of Indian dishes, and there are so many regional varieties that a whole book could be devoted just to this topic. Chutneys can be sweet or spicy, chunky or smooth, and typically incorporate some combination of fruits, herbs, and vegetables. As with most recipes in this book, the chutney and its significance on the table varies from region to region of India.

Raita is the most basic of Indian salads. It balances out the sharpness of flavors in an Indian meal and functions as a palate cooler.

Thengai Chutney
Coconut Chutney

———

Coconut Chutney is another South Indian classic. These days with the availability of frozen coconut it is much easier to make. Coconut Chutney can be served along with or instead of Savory Tomato Onion Chutney (page 233).

MAKES	TOTAL TIME: 5 MINUTES	DIETARY
1½ cups	Prep Time: 4 minutes Tempering Time: 1 minute	

INGREDIENTS

1 cup fresh or frozen grated coconut

1-inch piece ginger, peeled

3 green chilies

¼ cup blanched unsalted peanuts

1 cup plain yogurt

1 teaspoon salt

1 tablespoon oil

1 teaspoon mustard seeds

1 or 2 whole dried red chilies

¼ teaspoon asafoetida

INSTRUCTIONS

1. Place the coconut, ginger, green chilies, peanuts, yogurt, and salt in a blender and blend until smooth. Place in a mixing bowl.

2. Heat the oil in a small skillet and add the mustard seeds and wait until they crackle. Stir in the dried red chilies and asafoetida. Mix into the chutney.

3. Store chutney in an airtight container in the refrigerator for up to 1 week.

> *Note:*
> This chutney, as well as the one on the next page, makes a perfect pairing with the idlis, dosas, and other breakfast dishes in Chapter 3.

Kara Chutney
Savory South Indian Tomato Onion Chutney

This chutney pairs well with Indian breakfast dishes. I personally find it a great addition to a sandwich, particularly a breakfast egg sandwich. It freezes well and will keep in the refrigerator for up to a week.

MAKES	TOTAL TIME: 10 MINUTES	DIETARY
1 cup	Prep Time: 5 minutes Pressure Cook: 1 minute Sauté Time: 2 minutes	

INGREDIENTS

3 tablespoons oil

1 large red onion, chopped

6 to 8 plum tomatoes, chopped

2 cloves garlic, chopped

1½ teaspoons salt

1 teaspoon sugar

1 teaspoon cayenne pepper powder

1 teaspoon mustard seeds

10 curry leaves

¼ teaspoon asafoetida

INSTRUCTIONS

1. Put 2 tablespoons of the oil, the red onion, tomatoes, garlic, salt, sugar, cayenne pepper powder, and 2 tablespoons of water in the Instant Pot®. Close the lid, and set on Manual Pressure for 1 minute.

2. When cooking time is complete, do a Quick Pressure Release. Open the lid, remove the mixture to a mixing bowl and let cool.

3. Once cool, blend the tomato mixture until smooth using an immersion blender.

4. In a small pan, heat the remaining 1 tablespoon oil and add the mustard seeds. When the seeds crackle, stir in the curry leaves and asafoetida. Pour over the chutney and mix well.

5. Store the chutney in a glass jar or airtight container in the refrigerator for 1 week or freeze for later use.

Tomator Chutney
Tomato and Kiwi Chutney

This chutney from the east coast, is found on both Bengali and Oriya tables. The tomato came to India with Portuguese traders, and the Bengalis—unsure what to do with it—turned it into a sweet and savory condiment. Adding kiwi fruit is my variation because it gives the chutney a nice color. This chutney is especially good with fish or chicken.

MAKES	TOTAL TIME: 20 MINUTES	DIETARY
¾ cup	Prep Time: 15 minutes Sauté Time: 3 minutes Pressure Cook (Low): 0 minutes	

INGREDIENTS

1 tablespoon oil (preferably mustard oil)

1 teaspoon nigella seeds or panch phoron

1 tablespoon minced ginger

1 teaspoon cayenne pepper powder

8 tomatoes, halved (about 2½ pounds)

2 green kiwis, peeled and quartered

¼ cup sugar

INSTRUCTIONS

1. Set the Instant Pot® to Sauté mode and heat the mustard oil. Add the nigella seeds or panch phoron and wait until they crackle. Press Cancel to turn off the Sauté mode and stir in the ginger, cayenne pepper powder, tomatoes, kiwis, sugar, and 2 tablespoons of water.

2. Close the lid, and set the Instant Pot® on Manual Low Pressure for 0 minutes. When cooking time is complete, do a Quick Pressure Release. Open the lid, cool and serve.

Sweet and Tangy Pineapple Chutney

There are many variations to this Bengali chutney. It is more than just a condiment, and usually makes the transition between sweet and savory items on the Bengali table. I use dried cranberries instead of the traditional raisins for this recipe, and actually enjoy this particular chutney with crackers and cheese as well. By allowing the sauce to cook for a few minutes, until it almost caramelizes, adds a very interesting dimension.

MAKES	TOTAL TIME: 15 MINUTES	DIETARY
1½ cups	Prep Time: 7 minutes Pressure Cook (Low): 2 minute Sauté Time: 5 minutes	

INGREDIENTS

1 tablespoon oil, preferably mustard oil

½ teaspoon panch phoron (Bengali Five Spice Blend)

2 whole dried red chilies

1 cup diced pineapple

1 or 2 tablespoons raisins or dried cranberries

½ cup sugar

1½ tablespoons minced fresh ginger

1½ tablespoons fresh lemon juice

½ teaspoon cumin seeds

½ teaspoon black peppercorns

2 or 3 whole cloves

½-inch piece cinnamon stick

> *Note:*
>
> This chutney is great with any of the rice dishes featured earlier in the book, and can be enjoyed chopped as a relish with sandwiches.

INSTRUCTIONS

1. Set the Instant Pot® to Sauté mode and heat the oil. After a minute stir in the panch phoron, dried red chilies, pineapple, raisins or dried cranberries, sugar, ginger, lemon juice, and ¼ cup of water.

2. Press Cancel to turn off the Sauté mode. Close the lid and set the Instant Pot® on Manual Low Pressure for 2 minutes.

3. When cooking time is complete, do a Quick Pressure Release. Remove cover and set the Instant Pot® onto Sauté mode and allow the sauce to cook until it thickens and turns dark and caramel colored. Put the chutney in a mixing bowl.

4. In a small pan on medium heat on the stovetop, dry roast the cumin seeds, peppercorns, cloves, and cinnamon stick until very fragrant and somewhat dark. Allow the roasted spices to cool, then use a spice mill or coffee grinder to blend to a powder. Mix into the chutney. Let the chutney sit for a while to allow the flavors to settle.

5. The chutney can be stored in an airtight container in the refrigerator for about one week.

Raita
Indian Yogurt Salad

Raita is well-seasoned yogurt sauce and serves as a balance to the myriad spicy flavors of many Indian meals. Traditional raita originates from northern India. Much like the lassi, another yogurt-based favorite, raitas come in an assortment of flavors. Here is a basic recipe with four different variations.

MAKES

1½ cups

DIETARY

INGREDIENTS

1½ cups plain yogurt

1 teaspoon salt

1 teaspoon chaat masala

1 teaspoon sugar

INSTRUCTIONS

1. Combine all the ingredients in a mixing bowl.

2. Stir in your choice of vegetables (see below).

RAITA VARIATIONS

Potato and Mint Raita: Add 2 boiled potatoes, peeled and chopped, 1 teaspoon dried mint, and ½ teaspoon black pepper.

Beet Raita: Add 2 beets, peeled, cooked, and chopped.

Tomato and Red Onion Raita: Add 2 tomatoes, chopped, and 1 medium red onion, chopped.

Cucumber Raita: Peel and grate 1 large English cucumber and add to the raita.

Milagu Podi
South Indian Pepper Powder

Milagu Podi, which literally translates to "pepper powder," is an innovation from the South Indian kitchen. These podis are an essential shelf stable, and are an excellent accent to typical meals of rice and lentils served with the obligatory dollop of ghee, or enjoyed over freshly steamed idlis. I often spoon this over dosas (page 47), especially with some melted cheese.

MAKES	TOTAL TIME: 5 MINUTES	DIETARY
¾ cups	Prep Time: 2 minutes Sauté Time: 3 minutes	

INGREDIENTS

1 tablespoon oil

½ cup split Bengal gram lentils (chana dal)

½ cup white split lentils (white urad dal)

½ teaspoon asafoetida

15 whole dried red chilies

2 tablespoons coriander seeds

2 tablespoons cumin seeds

⅓ cup sesame seeds

2 teaspoons brown sugar or powdered jaggery

1 tablespoon dried mango powder (amchur powder)

INSTRUCTIONS

1. Heat the oil in a small pan and stir in the lentils/dals, asafoetida, dried red chilies, coriander seeds, and cumin seeds and roast until gently browned and fragrant. Stir in the sesame seeds, brown sugar, and mango powder.

2. Remove from heat and allow to cool slightly. Grind to a powder using a spice mill or coffee grinder. Store the chutney powder in an airtight jar in a cool, dry place. Serve with hot idlis (page 43) or any dal.

Index

Laal Maas (Rajasthan Red Lamb Curry) 198
Meetha Lassi (Sweet Yogurt Drink) 228
Mishti Doi (Sweetened Yogurt) 221
Namkeen Lassi (Savory Yogurt Drink) 228
Pahari Kadhi (Chickpea and Yogurt Soup) 109
Raita (Indian Yogurt Salad) 239
Tayir Shadum (Yogurt Rice) 67
Thengai Chutney (Coconut Chutney) 232

ZUCCHINI. *See* SQUASH

About the Author

Rinku Bhattacharya is a Gourmand Award-winning cookbook author, blogger and cooking instructor. She is author of *Bengali Five Spices Chronicles* and *Spices & Seasons: Simple, Sustainable Indian Flavors*, both published by Hippocrene Books. She resides in the Hudson Valley area of New York. Visit her at SpiceChronicles.com.